MW00637895

From Cornered To Corner Office

Overcoming The Most Unexpected Obstacles
That Stand Between You And Your Career Dreams

David W. Hults
CEO of activ:8 career coaching

W. L. Nelson Press

FROM CORNERED TO CORNER OFFICE:

Overcoming The Most Unexpected Obstacles
That Stand Between You And Your Career Dreams

By David W. Hults, CEO of activ:8 career coaching

Published by W. L. Nelson Press
St. Louis, Missouri

Copyright December 2006 by W. L. Nelson Press
9000 Middlewood Court
St. Louis, Missouri 63127
314-966-3888
www.activ8careers.com

Printed in USA

ISBN-13 978-0-9790494-0-8
ISBN-10 0-9790494-0-7

DEDICATION

To Brad Fuller, who encourages me to live out my passion, and who has taught me that immeasurable joy in life comes to you when you give it away.

To Jon and Judy Nelson, who speak with wisdom, who trust me, and who are committed to standing in the gap no matter what life may bring.

To the memory of Roy L. Wade, who taught me as a young boy that making mistakes is a part of life – and that no matter the outcome, it does not define your value.

ACKNOWLEDGEMENTS

The following individuals supported me tremendously in the adventure of writing this book. Their contributions – not just to this book, but to my career and life – have enriched me and my work. I am forever grateful.

Mary Berry	*Marilyn Lustgarten*
Elaine Bonzon	*Susan Margherita*
Darren Carter	*Michele Milosevich*
Nanka Castulik	*Judy Nelson*
Carol Cockriel	*Joyce Nichols*
Cynthia Cooper	*Patrick Niedringhaus*
Kim Cox	*Karen Sauder*
Rob Donaldson	*Susan Smith*
Deborah Dulin	*Nancy Toivonen*
Andrea Frazier	*Travis Ulmer*
Steve Fredrick	*Patricia Vogelsang*
Kathy Irish	*Dan Weber*
Guy Jacobs	*Trish Weber*
Shelli Kramer	*Carol Weisman*
Don Krohn	*Sharon Westall*
Sherry Lappe	*Joan Williams*

Author's Note:
Names and ethnicities used in this book have been changed to protect the privacy of the individuals included. The stories are all true and used with permission.

SPECIAL THANKS

The Survey Institute
Don Bruns, President

Founded in 1999, The Survey Institute is a full-service metrics organization that is capable of conducting an entire survey research project from start to finish. Their mission is to convert research data into meaningful information for decision-making support. That means that The Survey Institute can decrease uncertainty in business environments by converting data into valuable information, ensuring that every client receives insight on top of data. There is Ph.D. involvement in every step of the process to ensure that each project is focused and scientifically sound. To learn more about The Survey Institute and what they can do for you, please visit www.surveyinstitute.com.

Author's Note:
All data in each section of this book is provided by The Survey Institute of Wentzville, Missouri.

From Cornered To Corner Office

TABLE OF CONTENTS

Introduction

From Career Maze To Career
Amazement: Promoting Yourself
To CEO Of Your Own Career

Since 1987 I've spent time with executives and professionals in the area of career development, working to save money for the company and reducing the risk of legal liabilities. But in January of 2003, I made the most satisfying career move of my life: I founded my own business, activ:8 career coaching. Providing one-on-one career assistance to others and managing my own one-man firm fulfills me so much more than any old "job" ever did or could. Not only am I quite literally a CEO, I'm also, figuratively speaking, the chief executive officer of my own career. I'm singularly responsible for guiding my work through the inevitable highs and lows, the stalls and the sticky points, towards ever-reaching success. Likewise, I've carved out my own corner office that matches the figurative corner office of my dreams – a room of my house with a lovely view of the front yard, formerly used to store books and pay the inevitable monthly bills. This isn't "just a job." It's my livelihood.

And the highlight of my livelihood is helping people like you figure out how to do the same – to realize that whether you're the big chief, the lowly assistant, the field worker, the contractor, or anywhere else along your career path – you, too, are singularly responsible for making your career all that you want it to be. In other words, you're responsible for making your eight-hour workday work for you.

Though my work is so much more than just a job, it is far, far, *far* from the only job I've ever had. I've endured countless situations where I've felt stuck, stalled and confused in my career, not knowing what to do next or how to get there. In earlier parts of my life, I made about a dozen different career moves – some gratifying, others underwhelming, but every one of them teaching me something valuable about my career, and bringing me closer to the here and now – before I made the one that got me where I am today.

While I'm of course glad to have learned all that I learned, part of my work as a career coach is to spare you some of the setbacks, to teach you smart solutions to the universal problems you'll inevitably encounter during your career. Some of these setbacks will seem like huge and insurmountable quandaries, others merely annoying hindrances. But for all of them, there are creative ways out of the corner.

I embarked on my first career before I was old enough to drive: I was a singer. As a youngster, I occasionally performed vocal solos at church and school recitals. In attendance at one of these performances was an elderly woman who had been a professional opera singer. She said she recognized a hidden talent in me, and to coax it out, offered me free vocal lessons.

Mrs. Buenger proved to be a strict teacher; when I didn't breathe from my diaphragm properly, she'd punch me in the stomach. But her interest in me was also a huge turning point in my young life. Since starting school, I'd been unknowingly battling dyslexia and color blindness. I would not be officially diagnosed with both conditions until later in life. My academic studies at the time were a huge source of frustration and embarrassment, especially since I didn't even know why things were so much more difficult for me than they were for other kids.

Singing became an escape from feeling inadequate in other areas of my life, and Mrs. Buenger really made me feel like I had, and was, something special.

To this day, I still believe that our single biggest ally in building a satisfying career is self-worth. If you don't possess self-worth then, quite frankly, you are setting yourself up for failure. Opportunists will detect your poor self-esteem, prey upon it, and use it as a target for their own insecurities and a tool for their own betterment. Office politics will prove much more difficult for you to handle. Career advancement may elude you, even if you can't quite pinpoint why. But once you understand how valuable you are and truly embrace your own value, others will have no choice but to treat you valuably as well. (Think about it – did most CEOs get where they are today by doubting and undervaluing themselves? Definitely not.)

Our second greatest career-boosting ally, and too often our single biggest roadblock, is relationships with other people. What is going to make you miserable at the office? Undermine your self-confidence? Most of the time, it's bad relationships with other people. What is going to get you to the next level? Show you the way? Help you network the important connections? Healthy, mutually beneficial relationships with others.

That was exactly the kind of positive support I received from Mrs. Buenger. Armed with my newfound self-image, I formed a singing group with my two younger sisters and appointed myself our de facto manager. I lined up gigs, negotiated fees, chose our music and ran our rehearsals. We began performing during Sunday services and became a pretty big hit with many churches, all before I turned eighteen.

Given my love of singing, I decided to matriculate at a private university in central Missouri as a voice/piano major. I wound up only staying one year though, when I realized that I'd either have to become a music teacher (which I didn't want to do) or a performer (which seemed like a very rough career path). I returned home to St. Louis and managed a bicycle shop while earning an associate's degree in OSHA (government regulation and safety technology) from a local community college.

I still didn't know what I wanted to do with my life, so I enrolled in a college apprenticeship program in which students like me would shadow professionals in different industries. At my first apprenticeship, I spent some time with a juvenile court judge in Peoria, Illinois, sitting in his courtroom and observing him at work. But I found that choice of career a little upsetting. Sometimes defendants would be represented by state-appointed attorneys who would have to argue a case even if they knew their client was guilty. I also saw defendants get hauled in who just didn't care whether or not they got sentenced to prison. I came to discover that I personally couldn't handle a career where the apathy was so overwhelming.

Next I went to Arkansas, where I lived with a very wealthy business-man who owned a poultry farm. I was supposed to help him develop a benefits package for his employees. But I quickly realized that all he really wanted was a hired hand to help out on his poultry farm – and his brother's cattle farm. I only stayed there four months.

My next and final stop in the apprenticeship program was Chicago, at a place called Institute in Basic Youth Conflict, which ran seminars in cities nationwide for families and troubled teens. During my first three days on the job, they taught me how to drive a CL 9000 Ford semi truck. For the next three years, I drove one of the semis in their fleet, working as a paid apprentice and traveling cross-country from seminar to seminar with all the needed sales materials, set pieces and video equipment.

Upon arrival at each seminar site, I'd change out of my trucking clothes (company polo and khakis) and into my shirt and tie to train volunteers. Most seminars were run by a core staff of five employees, along with 40 to 50 volunteers in each new city. Attendance at these seminars would often climb into the thousands, and there were always different combinations of employees staffing each seminar. As I'm sure you can imagine, that meant there were always different personality clashes as well. (I could go into detail, but then this book would total a few hundred extra pages.)

Since I was one of the younger staffers, some of the managers began asking me to speak at little breakout sessions with the teens, where I'd talk about my personal history, my school and work background, and give a testimonial about what I'd learned in life. I'd talk to groups as small as 20 people or as large as 300. Through these breakouts, word about my singing background got out. The next thing I knew, in addition to speaking at the breakouts, I was being asked to sing at local churches during Sunday services. I also once mentioned to some co-workers that I knew how to cut hair, so they started asking me for trims during downtime.

How the heck did I know how to cut hair? When my two sisters and I were growing up, my mother wanted us to learn as many skills as possible using our hands. She believed that a well-rounded person was always learning new skills and had something useful to offer, no matter where life's journey might take them. The more skills a person has, she reasoned, the more valuable that person is to others. As children, my two sisters and I learned how to cut lawns, change a car's oil, arrange flowers and decorate cakes. (Our gender didn't matter; all three of us learned skills that could be considered "for boys" or "for girls.")

I had an aunt who was a beautician, and before I left for college, she taught me how to cut hair. I learned just the basics of the craft, and the most basic thing I learned was that I wouldn't want to cut hair as a profession. But I enjoyed the learning of it all the same because it spoke to my creative side, and because cutting the hair of my fellow students at college paid for my laundry. I was equally popular with my co-workers at the seminars, for whom I cut hair free of charge.

Acquiring new skills and expanding your horizons are two things I still believe in today as key ways to enhance your career opportunities. Especially in today's fast-paced, technology-driven industries, it is so important to keep abreast of the forefront of your chosen career by learning new skills. I've coached clients who have shown up at my door after realizing that their field's ever-changing technology has left them behind in the dust. I've also worked with people who were too stubborn to learn new skills, and their careers stalled because of it.

After working at the seminars for about three years, I started to notice a need within the company. Those of us who were out on the road had no point person back at the Chicago headquarters, no company liaison. If a shipment of materials didn't arrive at the seminar site, there was no system in place to track it or to ship a replacement. If a video that was needed for a seminar was misplaced, we had no back-up copy. Sometimes there wasn't enough petty cash on site to cover basic expenses, or even to make change at the registration table.

One day I outlined these problems to my boss and practically overnight I was appointed the director of a new company department, Seminar Support Services. Instantly, I was back at headquarters and was handed the reins to a staff of five personnel. I began coordinating and developing better communication between those on the road and those at HQ. I handled problems like missing materials and petty cash. I was given two secretaries to handle truck permits, material orders and basic administrative work. I supervised the writing of a seminar employee handbook. (Do you think I ever would have happened into this fantastic next step of my career if I hadn't possessed the self-confidence to articulate my concerns in a helpful, productive way to my boss?)

Over the course of an average week, our company could have as many as six seminars taking place around the country, with thousands in attendance at each. My department's work could therefore be very stressful. I began to see that, if I wanted things to run smoothly, I had to staff seminar teams with the right mix of personalities.

Our work soon started resembling a human resources department in miniature. Besides figuring out personality matches, one of my main duties was writing policies and procedures about how to handle mishaps or how to coordinate schedules. This was my first "aha!" moment, when I discovered that I really loved doing this. I really loved devising processes and building teams that would get things accomplished. I realized the field I should move toward was HR.

But I had no educational background in that field, so I decided to leave my job in Chicago and return to St. Louis once more. I took two years of courses at Webster University and earned my bachelor's degree in Human Resources/Business Management.

After I completed my degree, I encountered yet another obstacle along my career path: I had no idea how to crack the human resources field. A friend turned me on to a "career management" company. I'd never heard of such a thing before and until then, it had never occurred to me that somebody could make a career out of helping others with theirs.

The career management company helped me identify my key successes and strengths. This is much harder to do than you might think. We are all very good at listing our lesser qualities, the things we don't know how to do or aren't good at doing. Naming the things at which we excel, and doing so without resorting to clichéd resume-speak, is extremely difficult for most of us. But knowing and articulating our strengths is crucial when career conflicts arise. It also helps in finding or creating the corner offices of our dreams.

With guidance from the career management company, I soon landed my first job in human resources and launched my career in that industry, which I would stay in for the next 14 years. I had many different experiences in the field of human resources. Some were good, some bad. One of my most memorable experiences was when I was working as an HR Director for a nurse staffing agency. The nurses had dealt with other HR employees before, and felt that people like me didn't know anything about their profession. I decided to take steps to change that. Always looking to broaden my skills (and be good with my hands), I enrolled in a CPR course and got my CPR instructor's license. This gave me a tangible, relatable skill, a commonality to which nurses could connect. They began to work with me as if I were one of them. It also led to a new moonlighting gig for me as a CPR instructor.

For the next 10 years, I climbed the corporate ladder through several different positions in human resources, the last one at a Fortune 500 company. At that point, I began to examine the role of Vice President of Human Resources, and started questioning if this goal would ever be the right fit for me.

After lots of pondering and looking at others who were successful in this role, I realized that becoming a VP in HR would not match my strengths. Through the career counseling I'd already received, I knew what my strengths were: dealing with different personalities, building teams, writing policies and procedures. But in HR it felt like 40 percent of my job was crafting spreadsheets (that were rarely even looked at by my superiors) just to justify my being there, while the other 60 percent was about cutting back company expenses. Our HR team played the role of the stereotypical stay-at-home wife who tells her husband, "Look how much money I saved you today!" What had originally driven me towards HR was the opportunity to engage in creative team problem-solving. But the industry had changed, or at least the HR department at this

Fortune 500 company had. Now, it was about helping people just enough, but helping the company more.

Once again, I found myself hiring another career counselor to figure out the next move I should make. And in talking to her, I realized that I didn't just want her help. I wanted her *career*. I wanted to apply my talent for creative problem-solving to help people in this very specific and gratifying way. I wanted to take what I'd learned over the course of my career experiences and share those lessons with others, in the hope that they could also learn how to carve out a positive and fulfilling career and life.

While still working at my HR position, I began taking steps to obtain that career for myself. I defined my niche market: coaching clients from middle and upper management ranks, guiding them through unexpected career obstacles, transitions and ascensions. I started reconnecting with contacts who might prove helpful, and I discovered The Guild of Career Experts, a mastermind group of career coaches who could offer me support. After about six months of doing what I needed to do to get where I wanted to go, activ:8 career coaching was born.

I love that in my line of work, I focus strictly on a person's positives. My job is all about enhancing a client's career. (This is not at all like the job of a headhunter, whose goal first and foremost is to earn a commission, whether or not you really fit the job placement.) My work entails furthering a client's career opportunities by helping him or her discover, articulate, and position his or her value – positive goals that aren't reached by dwelling on negatives. Yet I know that, far too often, people allow negative influences to hold them back in their careers, oftentimes subconsciously without even realizing they're doing it. This is just one reason I have written this book: to demonstrate the positive, productive thoughts and actions that will best help you jump over career hurdles and get where you want to go.

And where you want to go – that "corner office of your dreams" – can be anywhere: running your own business, enrolling in a trade school, leaving the for-profit sector entirely, making a lateral move within your field, or advancing all the way up the ladder to CEO. This book will not tell you your "perfect job." (Although I will say, there are probably plenty of jobs out there in a wide array of industries that would suit you very well – many more than you might think.) Being the CEO of a Fortune 500 company may match your thirst for competition, your vision of big business, and your style of getting things done. Then again, you might be like our housekeeper, who is her own boss (in other words, her own CEO) but would never want to be another person's boss. She absolutely loves her job, and she does it quite well. (You can read more about our wonderful housekeeper and her past career woes in chapter four entitled "Paralyzed By The Unknown.")

What do the housekeeper and the CEO have in common? Both of them are going to encounter conflicts in their careers. Both of them are going to need to know how to recognize those conflicts before they grow too unmanageable and unbearable, and both are going to need creative yet practical ways to resolve these inevitable conflicts. That is what this book will help you do.

This is not a book to read through just once. It's not necessarily a book to read cover to cover, either. Take a look at the chapter titles in the table of contents, each one describing a particular career conflict. Which ones strike a nerve? Which ones sound like the issues you're facing right now – the specific ways you're feeling stuck, stalled or confused in your career? Flip to those chapters for more detailed descriptions of the problems at hand (each of which I've illustrated with a true-life tale from one of my colleagues or former clients) and an array of innovative solutions.

I recently took on a client who had worked at the same company for 30 years, making about $200,000 a year. He was just let go. Six months prior to his layoff, management at his company had undergone substantial changes. One day this man was chatting with a friend of his in management and said, "I know we're making all these changes within the company, but certainly I'll still have a place here." His friend didn't respond, a silence that my client should have interpreted as a sign that his job might be in jeopardy.

Instead, my client chose to ignore the signs. When he was informed that he was being let go, rather than being prepared and having a game plan ready to put into action, he was in utter shock.

This book is about reading the signs along the way. It's about taking the temperature of your career, your company, and your industry and predicting where and why problems may lie ahead.

In 2005, our country refused to read the signs forewarning us of Hurricane Katrina. We knew that a Category 4 or 5 hurricane was likely, and likely to head toward the Gulf Coast. We knew the levees in New Orleans would not be able to withstand such a storm. Yet we didn't read the signs, we didn't have a plan in place, and mass devastation occurred because of it.

Nobody ever thinks the disaster is going to happen to them. And that's the inherent danger of neglecting to read the signs.

If you don't learn from your mistakes, you'll repeat them.

If something's not working for you, you've got to figure out why it's not. And then look for lasting solutions to the problem.

If you're not satisfied with the results you've seen so far in building your career and moving it forward, or if you just find that your career pace has slowed recently, this book will help you identify the basic hurdles to career ownership, empowerment and success. The roadblocks that come between you and your "corner office" can be boiled down to one of four basic conflicts. You might be experiencing a conflict within yourself, in which certain self-worth issues or self-sabotaging patterns might be holding you back. You might be cornered by another person, such as a boss or colleague, who makes it extremely difficult for you to grow in your career. You might have issues with the technology used in your industry (which, again, is becoming more commonplace, considering how fast technologies develop and advance). Or you might feel cornered by the culture of your career – the kind of office environment you work in, or the nature of your field.

When I begin working with new clients, I take them through a very specific process that enhances their understanding of themselves, their talents, and their career potential. We start by pushing aside the resume, wiping away the job titles, and concentrating solely on the person's inner self. What energizes you? What do you do best? What are your true values, talents and interests that set you apart? After we've painted a clearer picture of the person's unique assets, we start to examine outward personality traits – how he interacts with others, what kinds of behaviors she exudes – and use that information to teach the person how to more effectively communicate with and manage a diverse array of personalities. This is critical to both the job-interviewing process and to the process of integrating successfully into a new workplace: learning how to read the "lay of the land," such as reporting structures and unwritten rules.

Next we look at the issues of technology and industry. If the technology has changed in your current industry, what do you have to do to grow with it? Which industries match your greatest assets, and will allow you to exercise your truest talents?

At this point, the client knows how to sell himself, how to articulate his worth, how to handle the interviewing process, and which industries to explore. The last piece of the puzzle is culture. What kind of culture is the best fit for you? Is it a small business or a large corporation? A company with a family feel or a go-getter attitude? Which prospective employers align with your values and your career profile?

To mirror my one-on-one coaching process, I've organized this book by those four subjects: Cornered By Self, Cornered By Others, Cornered By Industry, and Cornered By Culture. At the start of each of these four sections, you can read a little bit more about the nature of those conflicts. I've included some telling statistics on career satisfaction and dissatisfaction, courtesy of The Survey Institute, a St. Louis-based firm that specializes in strengthening employee- and company-wide satisfaction. The figures gathered by The Survey Institute represent more than 1.8 million American workers nationwide.

Within each of those sections, you'll find 45 specific, real-life conflicts that are most likely to occur during your career. The problems may be due to a boss who doesn't value you, a colleague who tries to sabotage you, or an industry that doesn't match your talents or values. After the root of each conflict is explained, I will offer concrete advice for cutting it off at the pass or diffusing it before it explodes.

Whatever the roadblock (or roadblocks), the outcome will always be the same. Either you'll figure out how to fix the problem (with which this book can help you), or you'll learn to live with the pain until it becomes too much to bear, and then you'll probably quit (or be fired, if your superiors are noticing your unhappiness on the job). One of my mantras as a career coach is "When the pain gets great enough, you'll change." That is a universal truth about jobs and careers. People will often tolerate near-unbearable work environments because the job is located close to home, or because the company has a good pension plan. I'm not here to chastise you for deciding to stay in a bad work situation. But believe me, when the pain gets great enough, you'll change.

Nobody's career is ever impervious to problems. There will be conflicts at your first job, and there will be conflicts at your last job. My career story is about working my way through conflicts, confusions and roadblocks until I got to a great place in my career. I've been personally motivated by that to write this book. In fact, this very book addresses a fork in my own career road that I identified a short time ago, which is how to grow my reach in the career-coaching field and expand my areas of expertise.

Whether you realize it yet or not, you *are* the CEO of your career. You're the boss. It's time to take control of your career like a CEO, and ask yourself where you want to go, and how you are going to get there.

Section 1:
Cornered By Self

1

H ere's the good news: According to research conducted by The Survey Institute, 85 percent of American workers say they are satisfied with their current place of employment.

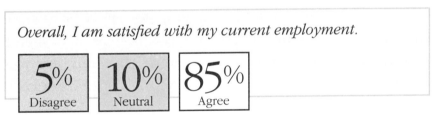

Overall, I am satisfied with my current employment.

5% Disagree   10% Neutral   85% Agree

But break that down into specifics, and there are some alarming figures. One-third of people polled do not believe that their current employer provides them with opportunities for career growth. Even more than that, a whopping two-thirds of workers surveyed say they don't receive the necessary training that would prepare them for these opportunities. And more than half believe that they don't receive adequate, regular feedback regarding their job performance.

I am provided opportunities for career growth.

16% Disagree **18**% Neutral **66**% Agree

I am satisfied with the training available to prepare me for other opportunities.

39% Disagree **31**% Neutral **30**% Agree

I get regular feedback on my job performance.

26% Disagree **26**% Neutral **48**% Agree

While these red flags point toward inadequate employee support on behalf of American companies, the crux of the issue is this: It is still your responsibility, as the captain of your own career ship, to make sure you get what you need. You've got to actively take charge of your career, because nobody else is responsible for taking care of you but you.

Depending on what issues are holding you back, that could mean erasing the old, self-devaluing tapes that run in your head, or it could mean changing those behavior patterns that keep you stuck in a rut. No matter what, it means standing up for yourself, speaking up for yourself, and sometimes going outside the norm of how people interact with their employers. Remember, even though you may have a boss, when it comes to your career, you are the boss.

Source: Statistics provided by The Survey Institute.

1 | *Not Knowing Your Strengths*

I chose to put this dilemma first and foremost for two reasons. One, it starts things off on a positive note, as it focuses on getting to know yourself better rather than figuring out how to handle other, often external and unpleasant, career roadblocks. Two, not fully knowing one's self and one's strengths is probably the single greatest career hurdle held in common by everybody out there who works for a living.

The number one way to avoid getting painted into a career corner is finding and knowing all the parts that make up the unique you! When you understand who you are, you can line yourself up with the industry, office, and boss that are best suited to you. (This also means that, ultimately, when you go on an interview, you can "interview" the company right back to see how good a fit *it* is for *you*.)

To illustrate my point about finding the unique you, I'd like to take you through the following diagram, which I learned from a training class I took years ago.

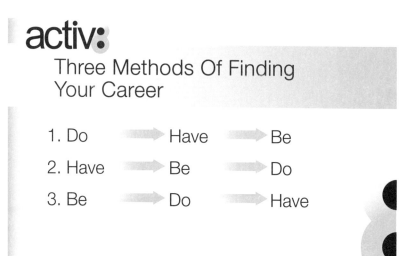

activ:

Three Methods Of Finding Your Career

1. Do ⟹ Have ⟹ Be
2. Have ⟹ Be ⟹ Do
3. Be ⟹ Do ⟹ Have

activ:8 career coaching

(Adapted from the work of John Scherer, The Scherer Center for Work and the Human Spirit.)

CAREER PATH #1: DO-HAVE-BE

We **do** things like babysit, cut grass, flip burgers, and wait on tables so that we can **have** a high school diploma or college degree. We then "**be** the degree" with purpose and passion, paying off all that we've worked for.

This is probably the most commonly traveled career path. Remedial jobs in our youth help pay for our education, and then we embark on a career in whatever it is we studied. Yet it's also the career path that leaves many of us feeling cornered. How many of us have come to discover that the degree didn't ultimately instill in us the purpose or passion we thought it would?

I know of one man, a pharmacist, who knew way back in third grade that a pharmacist was what he wanted to be when he grew up. But such lifelong conviction is rare.

If you don't know what you're about, then you're working strictly from an academic mind-set trying to find a career that matches your credentials, rather than trying to find a career that matches *you*, who and what you truly, inherently are. But you know what? You can have the most impressive degrees around and still wind up in a career or job where you get spit out on the floor – because the career didn't address who you really are.

CAREER PATH #2: HAVE-BE-DO

Some of us **have** many degrees (bachelor's, master's, doctorate) and/or many certifications so that we can **be** a doctor/lawyer/therapist/etc. We can then **do** this great work.

Some people think they need to stockpile all these certifications and diplomas in order to make their way toward the ultimate, satisfying career. They're the sort of people who take Career Path #2, detailed above, to an extreme. They may believe that education, in and of itself, is going to show them the way. Some of these people may complete years of rigorous schooling to become a doctor, professor or lawyer. Others may obtain the specific degree they need for a certain career, and then when that career doesn't fulfill them like they thought it would, jump back into school for a different degree and a different line of work. (We call this person the professional student!)

But a diploma cannot talk or think. A degree will not tell you who you are. A degree will not be the x-factor through which you finally figure out, "Oh, this is what I love to do! This is who I am!"

You can wind up a lawyer or a doctor and, as prestigious and lucrative as those careers are, still realize after all that education that you're in the wrong place. I know a friend of a friend, Dustin, who attended a top-name college where he majored in English. He also worked as a reporter and editor on the college paper, two endeavors that fueled his creative side. A couple years after graduation, he decided that the best career choice he could make was to attend law school. He got into Harvard, one of the toughest law schools in the country, where he wrote a column for the school's newspaper, as a hobby. After sweating through three years at Harvard, he spent the entire summer after graduation studying like mad to pass his bar exam. After that, he finally embarked on his law career, taking a position at the U. S. Department of Justice. He lasted less than two years. He is now a producer's assistant in Hollywood. Dustin always knew he was a creative person and was always looking for opportunities to feed that creativity. But he never let himself admit that law didn't address his creative side.

Education should be a tool used to enhance the real you, not to label the real you.

CAREER PATH #3: BE-DO-HAVE

Looking back at the last two career paths, we find that the "master plan" falls apart at "**be**." In both the hypothetical scenarios above, what leaves us flailing to find a good career fit is the "**be**" part, because we're not addressing who we really are.

So what if we started with **be**? That would mean identifying those parts of ourselves that just naturally are, that take no schooling, education, or career advancement to coax out. This can be difficult to do, because it goes against what society constantly reinforces as important. We are told that what's most important is *what* we do, not *how* we do it. But ask yourself what things you do out of habit. What are the things you do without even thinking about them? What parts of your work come to you most naturally? *How* do you do your work best?

"How" tells you what your style is. How you do something speaks to your being: who you really are, your natural self, the unique you.

So many career guides nowadays focus on the fact that, more and more, people just don't enjoy work like they used to. Why is that? Because we place no value on finding out at what we excel (that is, *how* we do things), or what excites us most.

Here is an example. What if I were talking to a classroom full of students, and I asked them to add together the numbers 3, 6, 9, 12 and 15? If it were me, I would be doing the math in longhand, and I'd still be carrying the two by the time several of the students raised their hands to let me know that the answer was 45... and that the numbers had a common denominator of 3... and that the square root of the sum was...

And then I'd ask, "Why are you doing more than what I asked you to do?" Their answer would be, "Well, doesn't everyone see this?" *No!*

Knowing your identity – your behaviors, reactions or responses – helps you determine the right career fit, one that matches how you work best. If you know yourself well, you don't have any misconceptions about your abilities, but you also know enough to draw more on your strengths than to take on a career that brings out your weaknesses.

And you also know that you need to hone in on those strengths that give you energy. We are all good at certain things that we don't particularly love doing. You may be great at mending clothes or filing paperwork, but that doesn't necessarily mean you love doing those things or would want to make a career out of them. When figuring out the unique you, focus on those things that you're not only strong at, but that you love doing and that give you energy.

When you know all this, you can say clearly and definitively, "I need a boss like this." "I work best in teams like that." "Here is the industry that will allow me to flourish and that energizes me."

When you find a career that matches how you work best, your boss will rarely have to ask you to carry out specific job details, because you are already on it, because doing such things comes to you naturally.

You **be**come the all-star employee because you know how to **do** your work in ways that grow the company. So then the boss looks for ways in which you can **have** more education and training to enhance the unique you and help you grow to your highest potential in your career!

Understanding this concept is key. It will help you manage your career through positive self-talk. It will help you identify the industry and the company that match your strengths.

activ: *Career Steps*

Get to know your personal profile. Personal profiling systems are tools that can help you hone in on your natural strengths. I recommend the DiSC profile and Myers Briggs. (You can link to a DiSC profile tool on my web site, www.activ8careers.com. The Myers Briggs profile is available at www.myersbriggs.org.)

Read books. I highly recommend Now, Discover Your Strengths *by Marcus Buckingham and Donald O. Clifton, and* Personality Puzzle *by Florence Littauer and Marita Littauer.*

Ask others to help you understand yourself better. Ask a few people who know you well to sit down and write you a letter outlining your strong points, the areas that need improvement, and the things they think you would need in a job or career in order to feel most satisfied in your work.

2 | *Not Knowing Your Weaknesses*

Usually, we know our weaknesses all too well. In fact, most people are much better at saying what they're bad at than what they excel in doing. But sometimes, when we have a goal in mind that we badly want to reach, we don't stop to think about how our inherent weaknesses might get in the way. We put blinders on and believe that if we just work hard at A, B and C, we'll reach our desired outcome. But it doesn't always work out that way.

Years ago, I worked in an HR department staffed with two administrative assistants. Both wanted to move forward in their careers, but each took a different approach to doing so. Unfortunately, both wound up with the same less-than-desired result.

John, one of the assistants, was a productive and helpful employee who was looking towards me to mentor him into a leading role that offered more autonomy. It was clear that John believed he'd reach the top by being a "hard worker," the employee who produces lots of widgets for the company. During the course of his six-month assistantship, John did take on some new roles and responsibilities, but he was always rough around the edges. He still lacked the maturity to see a project to completion on his own.

If John had talked to his boss about how he could best get ahead in the company, he might have learned that they weren't looking for somebody who was just a hard worker. That may be how John wanted to ascend the company ladder, but that doesn't mean it's what the company was looking for.

Sue was also working as an administrative assistant for our department. She was delightful at times, but she was also hampered by her own tendencies to speak in negatives around the office. She played the role of the stereotypical secretary who knew everybody else's business. She was also doggedly determined to get her B.A. in management within the next 18 months. She believed the degree would set her up for an instant promotion.

Both Sue and John ended up with the same outcome. John never could advance his career, not because he didn't have the degree, but because he didn't possess the "how-to" skills for the job he desired. Schooling itself wouldn't be able to train him to do what didn't come naturally for him; neither would simply exhibiting a can-do attitude. The fact was that John wasn't in touch with his strengths or his weaknesses. His self-perception was off, and he found himself grasping at straws. Sue, on the other hand, thought that doors would open the moment she received her diploma. She was sadly mistaken, and troubled because of it. She had no idea that she'd created a busybody reputation for herself within the company. Because of that reputation, no one would look at her for a management or leadership role.

activ: *Career Steps*

Never assume that you know the path to career advancement. Each workplace has its own methods of progression, and each employer has his or her own views on how you fit into that. Some companies care about educational degrees a lot; at other companies, the higher-ups may not possess any advanced degrees. Try to learn about the education and work backgrounds of the people above you to get a sense of what your company looks for in its employees. (Don't be afraid to just ask people about such things – people love to talk about themselves!)

Get your boss' input up front. Both John and Sue drafted a career plan without including the feedback of their director. Both of them should have talked about the required steps/mentoring/schooling and asked the right-fit questions before spending a lot of time and energy on improving their careers by making moves that produced zero results.

Ask yourself the hard questions. This is something you should do with the help of your boss. At performance-review meetings, or even at one-on-one meetings you request with your boss, pose such questions as: Do I possess the behaviors, skills and attitude to take on more responsibility? What am I lacking? Do you think that I have reached my potential in the field?

From Cornered To Corner Office

3 | *Being Too Good At Your Job*

It's one of the great ironies of work life: Sometimes you can be too good at your job, to the point where nobody else can ever picture you doing anything else.

That's what happened to Cassie. She was hired by a big hospital to work in its department of nursing education. Her original job description was a general one; she wasn't assigned to one particular task or project. Soon after she began working there though, she was asked to single-handedly redesign the hospital's nursing orientation program.

Cassie was, naturally, quite excited by the opportunity. She saw it as a way to make her mark and really define her value to the organization. Cassie's professional background as a nurse wasn't the only reason she was an ideal candidate to oversee the nursing orientation program. She also possessed natural talents for planning and organizing, for developing effective courses of action, and for mentoring and helping others.

So at first this was a great step in Cassie's career. She drew up an orientation program that was very well received by both the incoming nurses and the hospital administration, and she was regarded as a very good teacher. Cassie was so successful at implementing and teaching the program that she gave the four-day course once a month for more than five years.

During that time, she was also asked to create and administrate a second, broader orientation program, one for all new hospital employees. Teaching this orientation took up one additional day per month, so between the two programs, Cassie was designating one whole week out of her work month to teaching.

Originally, creating and implementing these orientation programs gave Cassie energy; she thrived on planning and developing. But in the long term, when the creation and implementation phases were over, Cassie wasn't a "maintenance" person. She didn't enjoy teaching the same programs over and over again, month in and month out. Not only did the repetition drain her energy, but it consumed so much of her time that she wasn't really able to keep her head up for other opportunities or areas of interest within the hospital.

Unfortunately, Cassie was at a point in her career where she didn't possess the confidence to speak up for herself. Her employers, meanwhile, operated as if in a "pigeonhole culture." They were typically reluctant to promote from within, believing that employees are well-placed where they already are. So when she was next asked to head the preceptor program – yet another orientation, this one focusing on the clinical side of nursing – she simply accepted.

While it was certainly flattering that Cassie's employers regarded her as a guru of orientation, the repetition ultimately left Cassie unmotivated. Cassie remained responsible for these orientations for more than 10 years, even though they never provided her with lasting satisfaction. It took her just that long to finally get up the gumption to secure a transfer out of the department.

activ: *Career Steps*

Learn the company quickly. When you're young in your career or new at a company, sometimes you don't know how a job works or functions; you don't know what's "the norm." That's why it's important to learn as much as you can as early as you can, not just about your position, but about the company landscape. What other options will you have in this company? Which other departments or positions do you think might intrigue, challenge and suit you down the road? Match this information with what you like to do and what you're good at doing, and you'll have a clearer picture of how you can advance in the company before you get stuck in a certain niche.

Make your mark, then make your stand. With her first orientation program, Cassie was just trying to carve her name in the company tree. She did that very successfully, but she neglected to take the next step by proactively saying to her superiors, "I think I can do this next." Instead, she passively allowed the company to define her rather than defining herself, and her natural talents and passions, to the company.

Learn how to recognize a "pigeonhole culture." Read about this on page 150.

4 | *Paralyzed By The Unknown*

or 25 years, Jill worked at a manufacturing plant that made parts for Caterpillar engines. Jill came from a generation and a familial background where they "didn't raise career women," which is why she wound up in a job that required no schooling, only basic motor skills. She never thought of herself as possessing any skills or abilities that could lead her into other career markets. She didn't know that there were other career options with real possibilities for her.

Every day at the plant, she had to prep her workstation before she started on the clock, lest she fall behind from the get-go and fail to meet her daily quota. (At most factories, there's an unspoken assumption that you don't need to prep. That's never true; it's just a way to eke extra work out of employees without paying them for it.) With only one 10-minute break and a half-hour for lunch, every workday was uneventful, save for the ever-pressing daily quotas. Working in the heat of summer and the cold of winter took its toll on Jill year after year. She often dreamed of leaving to find a new career, but the fear of the unknown and the need to keep her family fed made the risk too large to take. Jill would watch people come and go and often wondered whatever happened to them. Did they find a better career, or were they suffering financially? Were they endangering their families' futures, or was it Jill who was endangering her own future?

One day Jill heard that an office girl left her job to start her own cleaning business; she even had others working for her. This got Jill thinking more concretely about starting her own business, but just as quickly as those thoughts came, they were followed by a heavy wave of fear and doubt. She never let herself entertain her "what if?" notions and never even looked into what it would take to make such a jump herself.

Flash ahead five years. Jill received notice that the plant was closing and her job would be eliminated. A new, unexpected fear came upon her. Jill had never planned to do anything more than finish out her time at the plant until retirement. During her 25 years there, she'd been promoted from machine operator to quality inspector to team leader, but what was she to do now? It's not like openings for machine operators and quality inspectors could be found at every corner market.

Jill's financial severance package allowed her a few weeks to pull herself together. She found herself thinking once more of the girl who'd started her own cleaning business. If Jill had just quit to give herself time for career soul-searching, she wouldn't have received a severance package. But now she'd been pushed out of the nest with a bit of a financial parachute – so maybe it was time to try to fly on her own.

It was amazing what Jill learned about the housecleaning business in just a few short weeks. She found out about the going rates and learned about bonding and insuring her business. The more information she gathered, the more excited she became by the notion of starting her own cleaning business; she realized that this was actually within her grasp.

Flash ahead another three years. Jill not only has her own house-cleaning business, but has exceeded even her own wildest expectations in doing so. She can't believe how her quality of life has changed since the days of working in manufacturing. She loves the immediate payoff of housecleaning – not only the instant gratification that comes from seeing a pristine-clean house, but also the instant payment she receives, cold cash in hand. Life is 10 times better, says Jill, all because she made the decision to gather information and try something new.

activ: *Career Steps*

Get creative with your skills set. Working at a union factory for 25 years had turned Jill into an exact follower of deadlines and a punctual person, two traits crucial to showing up for housecleaning appointments on time and getting the job done in the time allotted for the task. She also possessed great motor skills, a natural fit for the housecleaning business. Your talents and skills would help make you successful in many different lines of work; you just have to think outside your own definition of yourself.

Empower yourself with the facts. Making assumptions about what you can and can't do without first finding out the facts will paralyze you. Commit to researching one question per day, or even per week, whose answer paints a clearer picture of your dream job. Seek out veterans in your dream field and do your research through them.

Make your dream vocation your avocation first. Jill might have started out by taking on a couple weekend clients, allowing her to keep her day job while testing out her new career goal.

She could have even offered to clean a few friends' houses free of charge in exchange for good word-of-mouth. There's always a clever, innovative way to dip your toe into a new career field. An aspiring interior designer could use a week-long vacation from her regular job to intern at a design firm. A pastry chef in the making could commit to making and selling cheesecakes or blackberry tarts (or another culinary specialty) at a food fair.

5 | *Shy About Speaking*

Jennifer was a smart woman in her mid-20s who worked very hard at her job as an associate editor at a magazine. It was a mid-level position, and she was aching to get a promotion to senior editor. She had lots of credentials working in her favor. She'd attended a top-ranked college, she had been at her current position for two years, and she was one of the few associate editors who got to write her own stories as well as edit others'.

A senior editor left the magazine at one point, and Jennifer felt she had a great chance at the job. Instead, it was given to another associate editor, Heather, who'd only been at the magazine nine months!

Jennifer silently fumed for weeks. At staff meetings, she couldn't stop herself from throwing icy stares in Heather's direction. But the more Jennifer watched how Heather conducted herself at meetings, the more she began to admire Heather's bold style of communicating. When Heather pitched story ideas at meetings, she didn't make excuses like, "This one isn't very good, but..." or "I'm not sure about this one, but...." She commented on others' ideas freely and openly, but without being overly critical. She even made suggestions directly to the editor in chief.

Jennifer realized that to get to the top level, she had to start talking like a top-level editor. She practiced pitching her story ideas beforehand so she could deliver them assuredly at meetings. She set herself a goal of making one unsolicited, constructive comment per staff meeting. Jennifer discovered an important tool for career advancement, learning by observing. She saw what kind of demeanor and attitude were needed to ascend to the next level and worked to adopt that attitude herself. She found out what the valued "currency" was at the office: speaking confidently and constructively.

Public speaking – whether delivering a speech, taking a turn reading aloud from a manual, or just asking a question during a seminar – is one of the deepest and most common fears people have. Yet that's also why it's one of the skills you must master in order to advance your career. Anybody who can project calm, confidence and authority while speaking in public will always be regarded with high esteem.

Eventually, Jennifer learned those things for herself and got her wish. The next senior editor position that opened up at the magazine went to her.

activ: *Career Steps*

Perform for the job you want, not the job you have. There used to be an old adage about "dressing for the job you want, not the job you have." These days, with all sorts of companies adopting more casual dress codes, that notion doesn't really apply anymore. But you should always act in a way that shows you're ready to take on the next level of responsibility. If you're in an assistant position, you can still conduct yourself in ways that befit a senior position. In Jennifer's case, that meant speaking up more at meetings and making suggestions for improving the company's product.

Make socializing part of your job description. Keeping your nose to the grindstone means, literally, keeping a low profile. Especially since communication was such a valued currency around the office, Jennifer should have made greater efforts to speak face-to-face with her superiors. An easy way to accomplish this is to eschew e-mail as a form of communication and actually make the walk to the workspace of the person with whom you need to speak.

Never underestimate the value of being a good speaker. Commit yourself to learning how to speak well in all kinds of situations, whether contributing at meetings, giving presentations, or having one-on-ones with the higher-ups. Groups like Toastmasters and the National Speakers' Association are great organizations that can help you improve in those areas.

Find your strongest speaking style. Some people do best when they're shooting from the hip. Others need to practice beforehand what they're going to say and how they're going to say it. Figure out what kind of preparation you may need to do (or not do) beforehand to deliver the best speaking performance on the job.

From Cornered To Corner Office

6 | *Working Dead-Speed-Ahead*

Darwin worked in Chicago for a large printing company, where he relished his position as a sales rep. He loved the glamour of working in the big city. He got caught up in the hustle and bustle of rubbing shoulders with the wealthy. He enjoyed his daily surroundings and loved feeling like a part of the inner circle.

What he didn't realize was just how much stress the job entailed. When Darwin started in the position, he was told that everyone received sales training, but that turned out to be untrue. (However, this is often very true of sales departments, especially ones that pay solely on commission.) He also quickly sensed that in this company's culture asking for help was frowned upon. (Another typical situation in commission-based sales: What motivates another person to help you out when there's no commission in it for them?) It's one thing to work hard; it's another thing to be immediately submersed into a job without being given a road map. No wonder Darwin likened the experience to joining the Army, where only the strongest survive.

Yet Darwin was smart enough to learn the ropes all on his own. In his mind, this meant he'd "passed the test," which made him proud. He'd figured things out, done his own troubleshooting, and succeeded. Rather than taking the company's "sink or swim" philosophy as a sign of trouble, he decided that, since he'd taught himself how to swim, he must be a good match for the company.

Opportunities abounded at this company, but with them came obstacles. The business was going through growing pains, which meant that new rules and processes were being enacted on a regular basis. One of the other sales reps was let go because he refused to align with these new practices. Darwin saw this as an opportunity; he took over the departing sales rep's territory, figuring it would increase his potential. In a way, Darwin was right. Within six months, he had increased his sales by a whopping 300 percent.

But Darwin neglected to foresee the sacrifice it would take to grow and maintain his "success." He was completely blindsided when he learned that he was responsible not only for his own increased field work, but also for the related administrative work being done back at office headquarters. That meant he had to manage people at the office even while he was on the road.

Darwin started to feel the stress of his overload. His health was poor and he found himself gaining weight and getting sick. Worst of all, he had a creeping realization that his life had become all work and no play. He just didn't pay attention to the amount of stress he was shouldering. He soon found himself caught in his job with no easy way out. For him to scale back would've sent a message throughout the company that he was "sinking" at the job, and probably would have resulted in his dismissal.

The only way Darwin could gain his life back was to leave the company entirely. This time he set out to read the signs along the way and decided to take the mountain step-by-step, instead of taking it by storm.

He found a sales position at a St. Louis-based company with a different incentive structure, where he figured he'd be able to strike a better work/life balance. Darwin decided to make the move and take the job.

activ: *Career Steps*

Don't worry about the Joneses. Almost everybody wants the penthouse view. And many of us enjoy feeling busy and productive, leading us to get caught up in always striving for more. But it's important to look at how things run behind the scenes, and how much we can tolerate. In Darwin's case, when another sales rep left, all he could see was the opportunity to take on more territory. Only after he made that commitment did he find out that he'd still be responsible for managing employees back at the office, which left him stretched to the limit. In retrospect, it wasn't worth it for Darwin to take on the extra territory.

Don't always "go with the flow." While it's wonderful when life presents us with unexpected opportunities, we must also take the time to stop and evaluate things, to decide how to create positive change for ourselves and not just wait for change to come. This way, we get a better sense of what we can handle, what new opportunities we'd really welcome, and what kind of balance we need to strike in order to be happy in all parts of our lives, not just our careers. It's never a bad idea to sleep on things for a night or a weekend, even if at first, the promotion or opportunity appears to have no downsides. Remember that you're in charge of your career, so you set the pace. (And if your company is pressuring you against sleeping on it, then what does that tell you about how competitive and impersonal the office culture is?)

Listen to your body. If you don't address your work/life imbalances on your own, your body will tell you all about them.

7 | *Fear Of Becoming "One Of Them"*

When Sun was in her twenties and early thirties, she possessed a healthy skepticism about people in management. Basically, she believed that managers didn't "get it," and she wasn't alone in thinking so. Her friends at work talked often about how managers were the "bad guys," people who made it difficult for those in lower-level positions, like Sun, to do their jobs. "Clueless" was another word Sun's co-workers used a lot to describe management.

So when Sun was approached by her employers (more than once) about being promoted to manager, she fought it tooth and nail. As time went on though, other factors started influencing her beliefs. For one thing, Sun was an ambitious person, and she knew she couldn't stay forever in a subordinate position. Sun also, like any of us, wanted to make more money. Most importantly, Sun came to realize that if she moved up in the company, she might be able to facilitate the relationship between the "worker bees" and management, helping each side to see the other's point of view and bringing them closer together in the process.

Sun was nervous about alienating her office friends once she finally accepted a managerial position. Much to her surprise, they all really supported her decision. They trusted her to bring about positive change, and they felt like they now had an opportunity to be better heard by management. In turn, Sun worked hard to be an approachable manager. She gained a reputation as someone who really listened to and addressed employee issues, rather than just paying lip service to them.

Sun still encounters many members of upper management who are oblivious when it comes to taking care of their employees, but every once in a while she comes across another manager who seems to "get it." Sun has also discovered new talents within herself. She now considers herself a good negotiator who knows how to draw on the strengths of her employees and colleagues in order to make a difference.

activ: *Career Steps*

Don't be afraid to challenge perceptions, including your own. I often say that in any workplace culture, perception is reality. Sun perceived all managers as clueless and difficult. Actually becoming a manager herself allowed Sun to see how a number of them really did care about their employees. Imagine the career opportunities she might have missed at her company if she'd never gained the confidence to make that uncertain leap.

Realize that with changes come good-byes. Whenever change occurs, good or bad, the first step towards incorporating it into the norm is to simply accept that to some extent, the identity and surroundings you know won't be the same anymore. This can of course be scary, but it almost always results in surprise benefits as well, such as when Sun's former colleagues voiced their unqualified support of her promotion.

Look for great ideas everywhere. One of Sun's strong points as a manager was her ability to listen for and seek out creativity and innovation from all employees. Anybody can have a great idea – a secretary, a receptionist, or your own assistant. Looking and listening for those great ideas is indeed part of a manager's job.

8 | *Stuck In A Job By Family Issues*

Carol waited until she was two months along before she revealed to her boss that she was pregnant with her first child. He replied flatly, "It figures."

This man was mere months away from retirement and counting the days until he could kiss his job good-bye. He couldn't have been more disconnected from his work or his team of employees. But toiling under a hollow, embittered boss was just one reason Carol felt completely stuck.

She needed to hang on to her health insurance during her pregnancy, of course. Her increasingly obvious pregnancy also made it unlikely she'd land a position elsewhere, should she choose to go on interviews. Who would hire someone only to watch her take an immediate maternity leave? (The federal law, FMLA, requires that an employer grant a woman 12 weeks' maternity leave and a guaranteed return to her job only applies if she's worked at the company for a year or more.)

After her son was born, Carol was forced to face these issues all over again. She and her husband, an Army doctor stationed at Fort Bragg, North Carolina, still needed two incomes to make ends meet. And interviewing for other jobs still didn't feel like a viable option, because now Carol's number-one priority was making as much time for her son as possible.

By the time Carol's maternity leave was up, her husband had six months left of his Army assignment. Then they could return to civilian life in the Midwest. To this day, Carol says that going back to work after Teddy was born was one of the most difficult things she's ever done. Ironically, she found herself in the same position as her curmudgeonly boss, counting the days until she could leave.

activ: *Career Steps*

Calculate the true profit from a second paycheck. When both parents work, more money may be coming into the household, but with that comes additional costs: commuting expenses for two, child care, two work wardrobes, perhaps moving into a higher tax bracket, etc. How much money would you actually net through two incomes? That's a key piece of information to have when weighing the pros and cons of careerhood vs. motherhood.

Demote your "career" down to a "job," at least in your head. Carol knew she just had to wait out her time at work until she moved with her family back to the Midwest. To keep her head up and her momentum forward-moving, she could have shifted her energy and focus away from this position and towards the search for a new one. Sometimes just doing your job and nothing more is enough, if your time and energy would be better spent planning for the future.

9 | *Running After Titles*

Diane always thought that the way to get ahead in her career was to stay with one company and work her way up. So during the five years she spent with a small graphic design firm, she continually documented her achievements and made sure management knew of her individual contributions to large, important accounts. She volunteered for tasks that nobody else wanted to do, she followed all the spoken and unspoken rules of the office, and she made it a priority to do whatever she could to keep company morale high.

Diane asked about being promoted on several occasions but was always told that, since it was a small company, the only way she could move up was if her boss, a department director, left. Eventually, Diane figured that the only way to grow in the company was to stake her own claim. She went to the president and asked that she be granted co-director status on a level with her boss.

The president agreed and said he would pass on the news to Diane's boss. Diane began to work independently, but before long, she started to wonder if the president had ever informed her (now former) boss of his decision. She knew for sure that he hadn't when she was called into his office and told to either follow the department director's orders or consider leaving.

The president never admitted that he'd agreed to promote Diane, who was shocked to be reprimanded by the very same person who'd granted her a promotion just a few weeks prior. Stunned, Diane agreed to "get in line," and immediately began looking for another job.

Diane finally realized that she was never going to get where she wanted to go by sticking with this company. Her experience and expertise weren't being recognized, and she wasn't being given what she deserved, even when she'd insisted upon it.

When she began looking for work at other companies, she assumed she'd have to make a lateral move into another designer position, rather than a director position. But she wound up landing a director position that also provided a substantial pay increase. Her new employer told her he recognized that at her previous job, she'd been doing director-level work all along.

activ: *Career Steps*

Beware the small size of small business. Diane refused to acknowledge the signs that there really wasn't room for her to grow upwards, with this particular employer. That's sometimes a hazard of working at a small ma-and-pa place of business, where growth often occurs slowly and the status quo is often highly valued. Unless the company happens to be going through an expansion phase, your career may also follow that status quo pattern.

Catalyze creative growth for your company. Diane was determined to earn a better title for herself no matter what the cost, and what it wound up costing her was that very title she so badly wanted. She should have focused instead on finding unique ways to increase her areas of expertise, such as asking for special assignments or volunteering to explore new areas of growth for the company. By building her skills set and experience, she could market herself more valuably in the future, whether to this same company or to a prospective new employer.

Don't copy titles. By asking to share her department director's title, Diane inadvertently made herself expendable, because how would it hurt the company to lose an extra director when they'd already survived just fine with only one?

Be willing to take a promotion without a pay raise, at least at first. At times, the career-forwarding wherewithal that comes with gaining skills and experience may ultimately benefit your career more than a pay increase, especially if you enjoy learning new things and finding ways to make yourself more marketable. If your employers tell you that they want to promote you but can't afford to pay you a raise right away, try to negotiate for one down the road. You might agree, for example, that you'll receive a percentage of the profits that come from the new growth you bring to the company.

10 | *Short-Sheeting Your Own Resume*

Matthew worked in the patient accounts department of a large doctors' office. A couple years after Matthew began working there, the department head position became available. Matthew didn't give much thought to applying for the opening because he assumed that he'd never qualify for it.

Well, guess what? The woman who wound up landing the job possessed no supervisory experience, had worked at the office for less time than Matthew had, and possessed less overall accounting experience. Do you know why she still got the job? Because she was the only person who applied for it!

activ: *Career Steps*

Market yourself based on how *you do your work, not* what *you've done. Just because Matthew never held a supervisor title doesn't mean that he possessed no ability to manage employees or supervise projects. His natural work style – the way he enjoyed showing the ropes to new colleagues, or his easy ability to prioritize tasks – could still prove very suitable to a higher-level position.*

Don't believe everything you read in the classifieds. Sometimes people don't bother to apply for a job because they don't meet every single little requirement listed in a want ad. But if your skills set and experience are comparable to what's being asked, it's absolutely in your best interest to send in a resume. Why? The prospective employer might not get as many candidates as hoped, or it may turn out that you have a networking "in" at that particular company.

Section 2:
Cornered By Others

From Cornered To Corner Office

Y ou probably don't need to read statistics on the subject to know that a workplace can come loaded with interpersonal problems. But here's some telling data all the same. Only 31 percent of American workers believe that their employers handle promotions fairly. Only 45 percent believe that their company recognizes employees who are excellent performers. Only 57 percent believe that they receive timely and meaningful information from management. Only about two out of three employees believe their bosses avoid playing favorites.

Promotions are handled fairly.

36% Disagree   **33**% Neutral   **31**% Agree

The company recognizes employees who are excellent performers.

22%	**33**%	**45**%
Disagree	Neutral	Agree

I receive timely and meaningful information from management.

16%	**27**%	**57**%
Disagree	Neutral	Agree

My supervisor does not play favorites.

14%	**19**%	**67**%
Disagree	Neutral	Agree

It can be very tricky to feel like you're really the CEO of your own career, the one in charge of your own success, when others you work with or for, colleagues or supervisors, seem to always stand in your way. This is why you've got to learn to play an active role, both around the office and in your career, rather than a passive one. In any job you take, you need to be having regular meetings with your manager about your goals and what you need to do to advance in your career. Find out what the measures of success are at your company, so you can always be setting yourself up to move forward.

If you're a good employee and you make your desires known, your boss will realize the need to create new opportunities for you so that the company can keep benefiting from your talents and values. If your superiors don't seem invested in that value, then at least you'll know when it's time to start looking for a company that will.

Source: Statistics provided by The Survey Institute.

11 | *The Micromanaging Boss*

Jacob enjoyed a passion for writing since he was a child. After completing journalism school and working for several newspapers, he was hired as a reporter for a weekly business publication. For many years, he worked closely with the editor there and won several journalism awards.

The business publication's publisher, Gail, was responsible for overseeing the general business and editorial operations of the paper. But it became evident to Jacob (as well as to others) that, in addition to focusing on overall strategies within the company, Gail felt it necessary to get involved in directing nearly every story that went into the publication. She came across as overbearing, demanding, and uncompromising. Though Jacob technically reported to the editor, Gail constantly bypassed this structure and took it upon herself to micromanage Jacob's every move.

Jacob's breaking point arrived when he was conducting an interview in the office with a well-known political figure. All of a sudden, Gail entered the room without introduction and interrupted the interview. She started criticizing Jacob's interviewing style, telling him what questions to ask as if the politician weren't right there in the room! Jacob was horrified and didn't know how he could possibly finish the interview and save face at the same time.

After this episode, Jacob decided that he had to approach Gail and express his frustration so that he could prevent something like this from ever happening again. For days, Jacob practiced verbalizing his concerns to Gail, combing over every prepared word so that he could address the problem without offending her.

Gail seemed to understand Jacob's concerns when he brought them up for discussion, and Jacob left the meeting thinking things had gone well. But soon after, Gail's micromanaging only intensified, and Jacob couldn't get through a day at work without facing intense scrutiny from Gail.

Even though Jacob loved the newspaper business, he knew he had to open himself up to other options if he was going to look for another job. Jacob found a position with a national brokerage firm in corporate communications that allowed him to use the same skills set he'd developed as a journalist. He escaped from working under Gail's microscope.

activ: *Career Steps*

Do not avoid conflicts. They'll never go away if you just ignore them. The problem might fade once in a while, but it will return unless there is a real resolve.

Believe in your abilities. Oftentimes in the case of a micromanaging boss, you have to do damage control in your head. Otherwise, self-doubt often creeps in as we keep hearing the criticism that makes us think we don't have much to offer. The longer you endure this kind of treatment, the harder it is for you to remain optimistic about yourself and other possible career options.

Look at ways you could transfer your strengths other than the current titles you have held in the past. Do some real brainstorming and then talk with others who are currently working in that new area of interest to find out if it matches your strengths and value.

12 | *The Boss Who Doesn't Care About Your Career*

Alice was a young woman in her 30s working at a foods company. She enjoyed her job and was highly regarded by her co-workers. At one point during Alice's tenure, her boss, Sally, gave a colleague of hers approval to go back to school courtesy of the company's MBA assistance program. Yet when Alice applied soon after for the same program, Sally denied her request. Alice couldn't understand why she wasn't allowed the same concession as her co-worker, since they worked in the same department and essentially did the same job. Alice went to the HR department looking for answers, but was told that the decision was solely at Sally's discretion.

Alice tried to brush the whole thing off and just keep on chugging at work, because it was such a good company and she enjoyed the work she was doing.

This is something I hear a lot from my clients. Many of us want to hang on to our title, or our enjoyable job duties – so much so that we kid ourselves into believing that if we just keep our noses to the grindstone and stay out of anybody's range of fire, we can keep moving along in our careers, or even advance in them. But by ignoring the signs – in Alice's case, the sign that her boss didn't have her career interests at heart – we're not staying in control of our careers. A better move is to look at other ways to initiate career advancement on your own, even if that ultimately means looking for a position elsewhere.

Not long after Sally denied Alice's request, she announced rather suddenly that she was leaving the company. Alice assumed, as did pretty much all of her colleagues, that she was the heir to Sally's throne and would be promoted accordingly; at that point, Alice had been with the company for five years, and all of her clients loved her. To Alice's horror, the department head above Sally replaced her with an employee from a different department – who happened to be Alice's best friend at work, and five years her junior!

Talk about feeling stuck! That was the straw that broke Alice's back. She soon left for another company. Six months later, she found out that the department head who had promoted her friend had retired. Does this mean that if Alice had stuck it out a little bit longer, things would have turned out differently at her old company? There's no guarantee. The important thing is that Alice took charge of her own career, rather than waiting for recognition that didn't look like it was ever going to come.

activ: *Career Steps*

Give your boss the benefit of the doubt. A boss can be a very nice person and employer, yet still not be mindful of your career. Sometimes bosses just have too much on their minds already, so it's up to you to put your agenda in front of them and make it part of his or her agenda. You will find out quickly whether your boss sees you as an important contributor who can provide long-term value to the company, or whether you are someone he or she has no intention of advancing.

Chart your career advancement as a team. Ask that you set up monthly or quarterly, one-on-one meetings with your boss where the two of you can draft up your career aspirations together – especially if, like Alice, you feel that you're working for someone who doesn't have your best career interests at heart or in mind. Make sure that the steps you discuss can help quantifiably measure your success and progress. When your annual review comes around, you will be well-equipped to talk about a raise, a promotion, or both!

Commit to open communication. This is critical if you want a long-standing position within an organization. I tell clients all the time that a boss will either make you or break you. Your success depends so much on the support you receive while doing your work. Strive for an open-door relationship with your boss, meaning that you both feel comfortable going in and out of each other's workspaces to talk about a project or problem. If you feel that you're not at that level yet with your boss, try this approach to improve the lines of communication: Repeat back to your boss any suggestions or instructions he or she gives you about work, and ask that he or she do the same when you convey information as well. This shows that you are committed to complete understanding between the two of you, plus it will help you better understand one another's styles of verbal communication.

Find something in common. Having a shared hobby or interest with your boss – one that's unrelated to work, whether it's a sport you both play or a TV show you both love – can help you develop a rapport of true caring. That human-relationship element of a boss-employee dynamic rarely gets the attention it deserves. You want your relationship with your boss to be about more than a mutual concern for the company's bottom line. True concern between the two of you as people will go a long way towards keeping your career goals on your boss' mind.

Ask direct questions. Alice should have found out the real reason why Sally didn't approve her schooling request. Was there a budget issue? Was Sally wary of losing such a good employee? Or did Sally really think that Alice just didn't deserve it? Going to the boss directly is always better than running to the human resources department.

13 | *The Sabotaging Co-Worker*

There may be times in your career when you encounter a co-worker who will do anything to discredit you, belittle you, or even try to corner you right out of a job. Take the case of Daniel, who worked for a leading Fortune 500 company. After he'd been there about a year, a temporary hire named Nancy was brought on board.

Daniel immediately felt like he couldn't trust Nancy. Even though she was just a temp, she acted like the queen bee. She quickly went about making everybody's business her business. Oftentimes she acted rudely and arrogantly right to people's faces.

Daniel wasn't alone in his suspicion. None of his colleagues liked Nancy – such consensus is almost always a clear sign that there's a poisonous co-worker among the group – and they all talked about how they found her dishonest and conniving. Soon she began coming in late and staying late, with the obvious goal of schmoozing up to the two senior directors who often logged 14-hour days. Since the end of the day is when people let their guard down, such a trick can prove fruitful. But there's a positive way to do it and a negative way to do it. It can be beneficial to use that time to improve person-to-person communication and to get a clearer sense of the boss' opinions and concerns. But with Nancy, Daniel and his co-workers suspected that she was attempting to improve her own profile by tarnishing the integrity of others.

All of Nancy's scheming ultimately resulted in somebody else's dismissal. One of the senior directors did a lot of her work remotely and wasn't always on the premises. Nancy capitalized on that by positioning herself as the person through whom this senior director got much of her information about what was happening at the office. She fed her insinuations about the person above her, Keith, until finally Keith was ushered out the door. Guess who took his job? Nancy!

The problem with these kinds of sabotaging co-workers is that they don't ever do their dirty work right in front of you. They have a keen ability to suck up to the leaders, managers and directors when you're not looking. Sometimes they will even take on some of the boss' work in order to be seen as the favorite employee.

Soon after Keith was let go, Daniel found himself in a dilemma. His department head asked him to do something that his immediate boss would never have allowed him to do. Nancy overheard Daniel's conversation with the department head and, as manipulators do, acted as if she could help in solving the problem. But while Daniel went to work coming up with a plan that would put a Band-Aid on the situation without offending his boss, Nancy quickly started portraying Daniel as an insubordinate who didn't follow the boss' orders.

By the time word got back to Daniel about Nancy's gossiping, his boss had already decided that he was guilty. Daniel was interrogated by his boss so much that he ultimately became fed up and quit. In the end, Daniel was angrier with his boss than he was with Nancy. He couldn't believe that his boss was clueless enough to take Nancy's side and that, since she did fall for it, she was even worse than Nancy was. Daniel felt he was better off being done with both of them.

activ: *Career Steps*

Take this great piece of advice I once received: "When someone shows you what they're like the first time, believe them!" If you keep giving people second chances to make a favorable impression, you're probably going to wind up getting hurt.

When you can't trust a co-worker, be careful what you share around him or her. Sometimes you can build a bridge through harmless office chitchat that will at least give you a minimal rapport, but most of the time you will not change the person's core behaviors.

Build a strong relationship with your boss. This is the best way to handle a sabotaging co-worker and prevent him or her from ruining your reputation. If your boss thinks highly of you and communicates well with you, he or she is likely to defend you to others and will seek out your side of the story.

Keep your boss abreast of your job. Daniel would have avoided most of this if he had shared with his director what he was planning to do when put in the awkward situation. If you ever have doubts about your decisions, do not hesitate to let your boss know so that it doesn't take him or her by surprise. Sometimes it's the very fact that it's a surprise that makes bosses think that things were handled incorrectly.

14 | *Torn Between Two Bosses*

O ne day at work, two female employees, both members of Ted's department, got into a shouting match at the office. This was no ordinary argument. It was an eruption the likes of which Ted had never witnessed on the job before. It stopped the day cold, causing everybody else to stand up from their desks and watch. In the hours and days that followed, word of the argument spread like wildfire throughout the entire office. Everybody wanted to know what had happened, and what was *going* to happen to the two women involved.

As head of the department, it was Ted's job to do *something* about it. And he knew he had to do something; taking no action would send a message to other employees that the company actually tolerated such inappropriate behavior. But before Ted could figure out the best course of action on his own, his immediate boss approached him and told him what she wanted him to do: find out who had started the shouting match, and fire her alone.

Then, before he could carry out her orders, the executive director – his boss' boss – told Ted to just fire them both.

Just like that, the problem between these two women became Ted's dilemma, one that could affect his career advancement down the road. If Ted handled the situation poorly, it would leave the impression that he wasn't cut out for upper management. If he chose to follow one boss' advice, he'd be badly damaging his relationship with the other. And if he didn't take any action quickly, he'd wind up angering both bosses.

The next day, Ted requested a sit-down meeting involving all three of them – himself, his boss, and his boss' boss. In requesting the meeting, he said to each boss individually, "I need you to help me figure out how to go about doing what you want me to do." Both bosses were happy to air their opinions in more detail and readily agreed to the meeting.

Once all three of them were in a room together, it didn't take much talking for the two bosses to realize how they'd put Ted in an impossible situation. There was no way he could carry out both sets of orders, since they were in direct opposition to one another. Instead, the three of them came up with a different approach. Ted would meet with every person who witnessed the incident between the two women. After hours of interviewing the staff, Ted discovered who initiated the argument. He reported his findings back to his bosses, and they agreed that only the initiator should be let go.

activ: *Career Steps*

When conflicts arise, face-to-face solutions work best. Once Ted was able to get his two bosses in a room together, they realized without any prodding from him that they'd put him in a bad position. Then they were more than happy to work with him to find a new solution. Imagine how much worse that process could have turned out if Ted had instead run back and forth from boss to boss, playing he-said-she-said.

Don't bring your problems to somebody else. Ted could have run to the HR department for a way out of his dilemma. But it's more efficient, and more responsible, to rely on the people who created the problem to help solve it.

Don't play the victim. Crying woe-is-me isn't focusing on a solution. It's just drawing more attention to the problem, and making you out to be someone who can't handle it. There's never a good time to play the victim, so just don't do it.

15 | *Breaking Through Stereotypes*

hen a regional sales manager position opened up at the electronics manufacturing company where she worked, Kelsey knew that her numbers were strong enough that she deserved a shot at it. The challenge would be to convince the VP making the final decision to give her that shot.

Kelsey was the only female member of the company's 14-person sales force, but her gender wasn't really the issue; it was her atypical selling style. The norm at this company was to adopt a rough, aggressive sales approach. Kelsey, on the other hand, believed in a soft sell. She excelled at creating relationships with buyers to make the sale, using more of a backdoor approach. She was aggressive, to be sure, but not at first. She preferred to first develop relationships with clients, then woo them into the sale.

Kelsey met with the VP, who, as Kelsey expected, voiced his concern that she might not do well with her increased territory and didn't fit the mold of a salesperson at that company. He asked, "Are you too soft?" and "How are you going to handle an aggressive client?"

Kelsey agreed with the VP that, indeed, she didn't fit the stereotype. But, she immediately followed, her approach still made a lot of sense. By developing friendships with her clients, she exhibited a high rate of repeat sales. By slipping sales talk into conversation on the golf course, she often convinced her clients to pick up a few extra units. Her friendly-rapport style worked well when it came to managing the upset client.

Kelsey got the job and exceeded all expectations.

activ: *Career Steps*

Know how to pitch yourself. Kelsey looked at her promotion from the VP's point of view. She anticipated what his objections might be, and prepared ready responses for them. Rather than butting heads about the merits of her unique sales style, she explained how her style could actually prove valuable to the company as an added benefit, not a potential hazard.

If at first you don't succeed, try, try again. Let's say Kelsey wasn't able to convince the VP that she was the right person for the position. Even if he'd chosen someone else for the job, Kelsey could've gone back to him and asked (in non-accusatory tones, of course), "What do you need from me to prove that I should be your next regional sales manager?" After finding out what those hurdles were, Kelsey would say, "Okay, I'll come back to you with your answers." She'd then make sure to stay in contact with the VP often, to measure the results of her progress. Show tenacity! Prove yourself! Go out on a limb and do it!

Be aware of the legal definitions of discrimination. Though Kelsey worked at a male-dominated company, her challenge was more about disproving stereotypes than it was about gender discrimination. If she and a male had applied for the same position, and she'd gotten an indication that she'd been evaluated differently than her male counterpart, then she may have had a legal matter on her hands. Legally, though, the burden of proof would have been on Kelsey to back up that claim.

16 | *The Absent Leader*

Keisha began her teaching career with a position teaching fourth grade in a public school district. At this school, all new teachers were assigned a "mentor teacher," someone with tenured experience who could show Keisha the ropes and give her advice when needed. Keisha initially took this mentor program as a good sign that the school's principal and administration cared about the welfare of its teachers.

Soon after the school year began, Keisha and many of her fellow teachers noticed that her classroom roll contained about one-third pre-identified "disciplinary problems." It was unheard of to give any teacher, especially a new one, so many difficult kids, and it was sure to make for a chaotic learning environment. Keisha's mentor teacher and other colleagues sympathized with her completely, but when she brought up the problem to the principal, he basically told her to deal with it herself.

After this encounter, Keisha realized that while the administration may have claimed to support its teachers, what that really meant was, "We support you, so long as you don't bring us too many problems." Though the principal surely recognized that Keisha was stuck in a no-win situation, he refused to work with her to figure out a solution. Keisha found out that the principal even kept track of how many kids each teacher sent to his office – a clear sign that her job could be in jeopardy if she relied on him too much for help.

That school year was extremely rough on Keisha; nothing she did seemed to be right or good enough. By the end of the year, she was a nervous wreck, unsure of anything she did.

The next year wasn't much better. There was an influx of fifth graders that year, as kids from lower-income neighborhoods were being bussed in as part of a Voluntary Transfer Student program. Keisha was therefore bumped up to a fifth-grade classroom, the most crowded classroom of the bunch, with the highest percentage of out-of-district transfer students. Many of the local parents suspected that Keisha's classroom was being set up as the "slow" one, and voiced their complaints to the principal and administration.

Even though Keisha's principal remembered quite well the problems she'd had the year before, he'd once again assigned her a difficult classroom situation and then didn't offer any help when parents started complaining.

That second year went from shaky to downright awful. By springtime, the administration decided to remove Keisha from her classroom. She was told to leave behind (for the substitute teacher) all her teaching tools and supplies, to make things look "as normal as possible" for the students, and was reassigned for the remainder of the year to the tutoring lab.

Keisha's union representative told her that her best exit strategy was to resign during the summer before contracts were issued for the next school year. That way, she could at least state on her resume that she quit rather than being let go.

Keisha left the school feeling very embittered about how she was treated. As a teacher, much of your workload is out of your control – you don't get to choose the number of students assigned to you, or which individual students you get. But Keisha also received no help from the principal, and found no alternative avenues through which she could appeal for assistance. The principal's hands-off management style showed that he didn't want to be a team leader. When Keisha needed a leader to help her through a difficult work situation, it was *her* career, not his, that suffered because of it.

activ: *Career Steps*

Find out where the support comes from, if anywhere. Keisha initially thought she was entering a caring environment because of the school's mentor-teacher program. But if she'd looked more closely, she might have spotted the roadblocks waiting ahead. There were no guidance counselors, special-ed instructors, or similar support staff on site to share the burden and help teachers when they needed it. All Keisha could rely on was the emotional support of her mentor and other colleagues, but it's not like they could leave their classrooms to go help her when she needed it.

Sometimes the best way to brace yourself for a fall is to simply accept that it's going to happen. Know that you're on your way out. Staying in denial will freeze you from taking productive steps. Once you embrace the change, you can take steps to make your departure happen more on your terms. Pep yourself up by remembering that at least now, you know never to let yourself sink that low again.

17 | *Forced Into A Career Change*

One morning an earthquake occurred inside Melody's kitchen. Melody was a stay-at-home mother for 25 years and was very active in volunteering and fund-raising. She had just sent her two teenage children off to their private school when her husband, a trial attorney specializing in construction law, walked into the kitchen and informed her that he had just filed for divorce.

Melody tried to steady herself as her husband continued. The divorce was not open to discussion and counseling was not an option. He was done and he was getting out. Which meant that, in an instant, Melody's decades-long career as a stay-at-home mother – specifically, her very necessary and challenging line of work as Executive Mom/Community Leader – was terminated.

Divorce is but one way you could be forced into a major career change. In fact, Melody's situation is similar to when a company goes bankrupt, and all of a sudden you've got to find a new job, new identity, new source of income – new everything, it seems. Even if Melody had held a part-time job outside of the home, her career would've been sent into a tailspin, since part-time jobs hardly ever make for a full-life paycheck. Situations like these aren't about getting unstuck from a dead-end job, or mustering up the courage to quit a job that's making you miserable. Earthquakes as big as Melody's are about survival.

There are many days when Melody feels cornered by a situation she didn't choose. She tries to combat those feelings by empowering herself with information. One of the first steps she took was to hire an expert who could calculate her chances of success reentering the paid workforce, and what kind of salary she could expect to earn. Melody has a marketing degree to fall back on, but still, it's been decades since she darkened the door of a corporate office. Chances are great that she won't be making the kind of money she would have if she'd stayed in the paid workforce throughout her child-rearing years.

This is a crucial piece of information for Melody as she negotiates her divorce settlement, which she needs to do before landing a job, so she can angle for as large a settlement as possible. She still doesn't know what line of work she'll wind up in, or whether she'll be able to continue living in her house, or even if she'll stay in the same town she's called home for almost 30 years. Those aren't decisions she can make yet, but she knows she'll have to when the time comes.

activ: *Career Steps*

Stop asking why and start asking what. When a trauma hits us, it's natural to ask why this had to happen. But there comes a time when sitting around asking why is no longer beneficial or healing. So the next question to focus on is what, *as in, what am I going to do now? What information do I need in order to move forward? What do I have and how can I use that to help me get through this?*

Focus on survival. Most of the advice in this book is about taking care of yourself: improving your career, making good things great. For a situation as dire and distressing as Melody's, who was completely blindsided by the news of her divorce, the first issue is survival. When you're just trying to survive, you work your way through the maze one small step at a time. How am I going to get dinner on the table for the kids tonight? Where can I stay until I find my own place? Who can recommend a good attorney? Think of psychologist Abraham Maslow's hierarchy of needs, the theory of motivation which states that a human's biological and safety needs (such as food, water and shelter) must first be met before you can address needs of love, esteem and belonging.

Open yourself up to discovery. After you've weathered the survival period and you're back on some kind of solid ground, it's time to start casting the career net. It can feel uneasy to go from the hunker-down mode of survival to the optimism of self-discovery, but it's a necessary step toward building your dream career from here on out. Think about options you've never considered before – selling the house, moving to another state – always backing up those ideas with fact-finding. When your foundation has crumbled and you're starting from scratch, you can actually rebuild in an infinite number of ways. What's your purpose now? What is it you really want?

18 | *Broken Down By A Broken Authority Structure*

Josh, an executive salesperson and account manager with a major wireless services company, really had to pat himself on the back when he landed the national corporate account he'd been pursuing for weeks. He'd courted his client extensively, promoting the numerous ways this customized wireless service package would help him better manage his time, team and money. Josh always prided himself on creating connections with other executives and developing win-win relationships. He also knew that making good on his word was critical to keeping the client and growing the account.

After he and the client signed off on the deal, Josh headed back to his office to get the ball rolling. There were two support staffers whose jobs were to execute the technical work necessary to customize the service package. Josh submitted a detailed work order and deadline, telling them, "We need to make sure this gets done on time."

Though the support team worked on Josh's accounts, he wasn't their boss. In fact, Josh and the support staffers shared the same boss. Even more confounding, the two support staffers were guaranteed a portion of Josh's sales commission even if they dropped the ball on their end of the project… which they did.

At one point during the implementation process, they needed the company president to sign off on a crucial step. When the president didn't return their call, they just let the project stall rather than take active steps to secure the president's authorization. The boss they shared with Josh also never bothered to step in and help solve the problem himself.

As soon as Josh found out about this, he got on the phone and conferenced in both the support staff and the president. Within minutes, he'd resolved the issue so the project could move forward. But by that point, Josh had to tell his client that they couldn't deliver his service package by the original, agreed-upon deadline.

Josh was majorly cornered in three ways by his company's hierarchy. One, it was hugely problematic that Josh's support staff didn't report to him directly. It prevented Josh from solving small problems before they became big ones. It also prevented him from issuing appropriate reprimands when support staffers messed up. Two, it was ridiculous that the company granted these support staffers a percentage of Josh's sales commission without requiring them to meet their deadlines. In essence, the company was telling them that they needn't take responsibility for their own work. Three, the boss' nonconfrontational style – not intervening early enough and letting Josh deal with problems on his own – meant that Josh was pretty much doing his boss' job as well as his own. All of these factors combined to negatively affect Josh's sales performance and overall productivity.

activ: *Career Steps*

Get your boss to buy into your job performance. Josh needs to demonstrate to his boss (in a way that doesn't make him appear insubordinate) how it benefits both of them to help one another. If the boss would act more aggressively in handling problems like those brought on by the support staff, then Josh would be able to better serve his clients, which would result in higher customer satisfaction ratings for the department.

Know when to say "we." When Josh told the support staffers that "we" needed to complete the work order on time, he inadvertently made himself partly responsible for their duties. Instead, he should have used the word "you." As in, "Will you keep me abreast of how this project develops?" Or, "You need to let me know if any problems surface on this work order." This way, the responsibility to carry out the task clearly lies with the support staffers.

Get the boss' buy-in on a big meeting. The "buy-in" is where you persuade your boss that by addressing your issues, he's really helping himself. You also need to convince him that he's the one driving this change-inducing meeting, because no boss wants to feel that an employee is being insubordinate. It would benefit Josh's boss to develop a process with built-in accountability because that would lead to higher customer satisfaction ratings for the department. Also, Josh won't be in this position forever, and the next account manager might not do as good a job as Josh at addressing problems when needed.

19 | *When The "Big Dog" Is Always Right*

When Marcus was promoted from senior production manager to associate production director at an advertising agency, he thought his opinion around the office would start to matter more. Before he received his promotion, it had appeared to him that upper management had more of a say in creating policy. What he didn't realize was that it wasn't your title that gave you a voice in this company, it was how much the president, and the president alone, valued your opinion.

Marcus tried to be a good associate director by passing along worthwhile ideas from his production team to the president. Not only did the president flatly reject every one of them, but at one point he even told Marcus, "We consider everyone replaceable." Another time, Marcus put together a proposal that would save the company significant amounts of money. The president told Marcus that he had no intention of reading it, and that the company "makes enough money."

That was the last straw for Marcus. He began looking for positions in companies that would value experience and insight, not just his, but that of everyone at the company.

activ: *Career Steps*

Build a right to be heard. Sometimes people think that once they reach a certain rank, they'll automatically receive more consideration from and communication with the top brass. But you might find even more bumps in the road by making that assumption. Building a relationship with this particular boss should have been a high priority on Marcus' to-do list once he received his promotion, understanding how his boss thinks and what drives him, so he could submit ideas that were more in line with his boss' beliefs.

Be wary of a no-win situation. If you and your boss are this different in both personality and values, your career might be short-lived at this particular company.

20 | *The Job Isn't What They Promised*

After sweating her way through a stressful work environment at a major public relations firm, Dana was incredibly excited to begin a new, high-level position at a sports marketing corporation. She had been told during the interview process that the job came with a lot of responsibility, which Dana felt more than ready to take on after proving herself through a series of high-profile projects at her last job. Not one full week after starting at the new company, Dana found out that "a lot of responsibility" was a euphemism for "cleaning up the last person's overwhelming mess." Dana didn't know why the last marketing exec had left, whether she'd quit or been fired. All Dana knew was that she found herself working 80-hour weeks with no end in sight.

Bill accepted a job as a software instructor at a major manufacturing corporation because he wanted a chance to work one-on-one with people as well as spend time working with computers. Instead, he found himself face-to-face with screen after screen, troubleshooting tedious PCs and network failures.

Sam was looking forward to the next step of his career, selling high-tech drafting equipment to architectural firms. That is, until his new boss encouraged him to deceive customers with false claims about their products' capabilities.

I've heard tons of woeful tales like these from my clients. They accept a new position at a new company with all the optimism in the world, only to quickly realize that the job at hand isn't the job they were promised.

It may seem like the only option is to quit, but there are constructive steps you can take to try to turn the job around.

activ: *Career Steps*

Give it six to 12 weeks. Those first couple months may not be a reliable indicator of the job, the workload, or the amount of responsibility your boss will ultimately give you. It usually takes about that long for a new employee to go through all formal and informal training. It also may be a time when your new boss is still gradually working you into things.

Tell your employer, "Help me help you." With her grueling schedule, Dana might be prone to making expensive mistakes. She could try to negotiate for an assistant to help shoulder her workload. Bill could point out to his boss that in spending so much time working just with computers, he's only doing half of the job he's capable of doing. Sam could point out that once he loses credibility with a customer, it's almost impossible to regain it, which would cost the company big dollars in the long term.

Always get your job description in writing. If you can, get one during the interviewing process, before the job is even formally offered to you. A written job description should contain six or seven key responsibilities. Any more than that is a strong indicator that the job will prove overwhelming. A written description will also help you prioritize your workload, and will protect your job from undergoing major changes if your boss ever leaves.

21 | *Working Alongside Incompetents*

J ane had long worked as a nurse in a Florida hospital. At one point during her tenure there, the department she worked in became short-staffed.

The hospital administration responded to this need by "importing" nurses from the Philippines. These nurses hadn't undergone the same rigorous training as the U.S.-educated nurses. Jane wasn't even sure if they possessed all the certifications and credentials required by state and federal law. Whether they did or not, neither the nursing staff nor the hospital's patients felt comfortable around them. At one point, Jane witnessed one of the new nurses remove a patient's IV by disconnecting the tube – but leaving the needle stuck in the patient's arm!

After news of that episode spread around the ward, many patients were ready to walk out. Jane and the other nurses had to start shadowing the new nurses on their rounds to make sure they did their jobs right, and that the patients were safe. This left the "old guard" nurses with less time on their shift to take care of their own work.

Jane was so stunned by this situation, she wasn't sure what to do. She wanted to voice her complaints and concerns as high up the ladder as she could, but she also had to devote most of her time and energy to just making sure the patients were safe and properly cared for on an hour-to-hour, day-to-day basis. She knew that it would be little use to complain to her managers or to human resources, since they were the people who'd hired these new nurses in the first place. She considered blowing the whistle on the hospital's questionable practices, but she didn't trust her own negotiating skills to do so and feared that it would put her career in danger.

activ: *Career Steps*

Figure out how to be a part of the solution. As much as Jane's hospital was in the wrong, Jane (and her colleagues) needed to take steps beyond just pointing this out to any higher-ups who would listen. It wasn't Jane's responsibility to single-handedly solve the nursing shortage, but perhaps if the staff put their collective heads together, they could've at least come up with options for adequately staffing the floor with competent, registered nurses.

When you have a license, protect it! For Jane and her co-workers, this issue wasn't just about being stretched on the job, or even just about potentially losing their jobs. Their licenses were at stake, especially if a patient negligence suit would ever be brought against the hospital. An appeal must be made wherever possible: to the administration, to the nurses union spokesperson, or to the hospital's board. It's also crucial to document all these appeals in writing. If there is still no change, Jane might have to seriously consider leaving, to protect her license if nothing else.

From Cornered To Corner Office

22 | *Overqualified And Underemployed*

Tim worked on a team with other Information System professionals and once found himself in a tight situation when a new manager was assigned to his particular team. There was new business coming into the company, so in addition to the new manager, two more full-time employees were being added to Tim's team to handle the increased workload.

Tim wanted to work toward assuming the role of project manager, but it didn't take long for him to find out that the new manager wasn't considering him for such increased responsibility. He was consistently assigned low-priority work with little real responsibility. In fact, after Tim did a little digging, he found out that every single one of his teammates had been given at least some project manager responsibilities – except for him!

Tim asked the manager why he wasn't given the same chance as the others. She said she was only handing out project manager titles to people with prior experience, but Tim knew that the amount of education and experience on his team was quite low. In fact, nobody on the team but Tim had a master's degree in computer systems.

Still, Tim persisted with his work on the team, but it did him no good. He was overlooked for two other key promotions until finally his manager was moved to another team. Her replacement quickly assessed Tim's abilities and reassigned him to work on higher-profile projects. Finally, Tim got the chances he was hoping for three years earlier.

activ: *Career Steps*

Switch teams in the beginning! There were so many other IS teams around Tim's office, not only could he have transferred to one of them, but he should have. Instead, Tim stuck it out and eventually (after three years) his luck changed; his team was assigned a new manager. But typically, it takes even longer for upper management to figure out that problems lie with middle management, not with workers below them.

Read your manager's cues. When your manager is hedging his or her answers to your questions about when you can expect to move forward, or what other skills or experience you need to be considered promotable, that's a very strong sign that real change and advancement are not going to come through this boss.

Sometimes you never get the why answered. As with Tim, his manager never really seemed to tell him the truth about why she didn't want to promote him. So instead, focus on new questions, and ask them of yourself. What do I do with the information I do have? What should I be doing to take control of the situation rather than becoming a victim?

23 | *Senior Officer Without A Say*

J oe loved his job as a senior financial officer at a prominent Midwestern bank. But every once in a while, he'd run into problems playing the "political game." For example, he once had to interview candidates for a new controller at his bank branch. He found an internal candidate from the bank's Kansas City office and was very impressed with her. Joe had the CEO at his branch conduct a second interview with her and he, too, was ready to hire her.

But the regional office, which wanted to look outside the company for new blood rather than hire from within, found an external candidate and told Joe to interview him as well.

As Joe was conducting the interview, he felt a disconnect with the candidate but couldn't quite put his finger on what it was he didn't like. The regional office didn't put much stock in Joe's concern, figuring he was just being difficult because he wanted to hire his own candidate.

After much prodding from the regional office, Joe reluctantly hired the outside candidate as the new controller. He turned out to be a disaster and was terminated within three months. Joe did eventually get to hire his own candidate, but only after waiting about four months while the regional office stalled to grant him permission. The regional office, it seemed, held its grudge for quite a while.

activ: *Career Steps*

Give specifics. The regional office didn't buy Joe's vague argument that there was "just something he didn't like" about the external candidate. He should have prodded more deeply during the interview to better identify the problem, even if it meant conducting a second interview. It's always better to speak in details and specifics during a politically charged discussion.

Join forces. Joe was right to ask his CEO to conduct a second interview with the internal candidate, but he shouldn't have stopped there. He could've asked the CEO to help interview the second candidate and to go to bat against the regional office with him. This would give the impression that it's not just Joe who has strong opinions for one candidate and against another.

From Cornered To Corner Office

24 | *Family Business Owner Trumps Your Vote*

Coretta, the vice president of a leading bank, hired several originators for the branch. Originators are schooled individuals who are experts in managing mortgage loans. The idea behind this new business venture was to provide a service that would bring added revenue into the bank. The plan was to build such a solid reputation for handling mortgage loans that customers would recognize an added value. The only problem was the impatience of the bank owner. He was looking for a faster return on a one-year investment. He and the other bank leaders crippled the new business venture by getting rid of the experts. And Coretta? He decided to have her train the personal bankers about how to process mortgage loans.

The Controller, COO, Senior Vice President Commercial Lending, Senior Vice President HR, and the CEO of the bank held a meeting at which they voted to get rid of all the originator positions (since the bank was paying a higher rate of pay for their expertise).

As Coretta's experience illustrates, senior management often makes decisions without talking to those whose input may be valuable.

Coretta voiced her concern about the change but found that she was the only one in favor of giving the business venture more time to develop and of keeping the experts on staff. The vote was taken and Coretta found herself singing solo. It was decided that Coretta's responsibilities would increase, including training her already stressed out personal bankers to process mortgage loans. Coretta left the meeting defeated and is questioning whether or not to remain with her present employer.

activ: *Career Steps*

Coretta felt that – even though she was allowed to speak in the meeting – no one really heard her. The decision was already made behind closed doors. This often happens when the owner or president of a company is driving the agenda. I've met so many people who want to get into business on their own because of this very thing called empowerment! When you get to call the shots and create your own rules, you alone have the power to control your company's destiny.

It's very important that Coretta understand three things: 1. What's in her circle of control (her autonomy). 2. What's in her circle of influence (could she have regularly kept the owner in the loop and highlighted positive outcomes, like customer satisfaction letters, referrals, etc.?). 3. What's outside her circle of control (she's not the owner, so there will be times that she can't control him or what the market will yield). Getting real with herself and knowing what it is that she can or cannot influence will help Coretta come to an understanding about whether or not this will be a lasting career position.

25 | *Escaping Questionable Practices*

Lynn worked in Florida on the accounting side of an international manufacturing company. She thrived within the company and was promoted twice. Yet Lynn had a growing concern about some of the accounting practices of the controller. It seems that he was manipulating numbers to personally benefit. What's worse, he was rewarded for watching and controlling big financial changes. Lynn was frustrated because his practices affected other employees within the company. As a result of the controller maneuvering the projected figures, a number of good employees lost their jobs!

Lynn soon found herself interviewing for a transfer to North Carolina. When the controller asked Lynn why she wanted to transfer, she hesitantly told him that she didn't agree with some of his accounting practices. The controller was not happy with the conversation, seemingly glad that she was on her way out the door. Lynn felt comforted by the fact that she escaped from having to work under someone who was – in her opinion – unethical.

The company paid for relocation and Lynn was well on her way to continuing with her career. Not long after she arrived, the controller in North Carolina resigned and a new controller was transferred in from, of all places, Florida! It didn't take long before he was back to his questionable accounting practices. Lynn found herself trapped since she couldn't transfer again so soon. Lynn felt forced to leave the company and subsequently found a new place to call home.

activ**:** *Career Steps*

Was the company really the right company for her if no one questioned the controller's behavior? You never know who is watching whom. The important thing was that Lynn read the signs along the way instead of being complacent. Wisely, she embraced the idea that change was inevitable.

But you must always remember to be careful about burning bridges. When the controller asked why she wanted to transfer after spending so much time and energy getting promoted, Lynn should have given a gracious answer. Most of the time when you feel tension within a working relationship, the other employee feels it as well. The right time to be honest about your working relationship is when both of you are willing to talk about it and no one is leaving their position.

Section 3:
Cornered By Industry

"When management tells me something, I believe it." The Survey Institute found that 59 percent of American workers agree with the above statement – not a very strong sign of people's faith in their jobs, their bosses, their companies, or even their fields of industry.

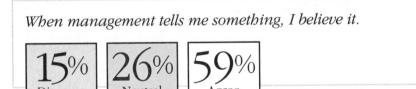

When management tells me something, I believe it.

15%	26%	59%
Disagree	Neutral	Agree

Clear, honest communication from management is a critical part of your career because change is the very nature of any industry. If you're not receiving good communication from management, it can make it more difficult to weather these changes over the course of your career.

Oftentimes, these changes are due to advancements in technology. If years and years ago you were a typesetter, you're not a typesetter today because that industry is gone; it's been replaced by computers. Or take a look at Blockbuster. That corporation was dominant in its market, until

Netflix came along and changed the market's nature altogether. Blockbuster had to scramble to change its business model in order to keep up.

Sometimes a company will recognize change early on and step up to the challenge of keeping ahead of the status quo. Other times, a company may be in denial. It's your job to examine how your company addresses these things, and how they address their employees about changes. This way you'll know how secure your position is within both the company and the industry.

Sixty-nine percent of workers polled by The Survey Institute believe that their company is sincere when it emphasizes quality of product and customer service. This is another important statistic. If your company doesn't care about the quality of its work, then how much does it really care about the quality of your individual work, your true talents and passions?

My company is sincere when it emphasizes quality of products and customer service.

10%	21%	69%
Disagree	Neutral	Agree

Source: Statistics provided by The Survey Institute.

26 | *Falling Behind The Techno-Times*

Betsy worked as an ultrasound technician for a well-known hospital in the Midwest. After four years on the job, she started reading in trade publications about significant technological advancements that were being made in her line of work – advancements that would require her to undergo additional training. In order to remain marketable, Betsy needed to learn the new technology of 3D/4D Ultrasound.

The hospital that employed Betsy wasn't offering any 3D/4D training, so she talked to her co-workers about it in an attempt to "rally the troops." She figured if enough of them got enthused about new training, they could pressure the hospital into providing it; barring that, perhaps they could seek outside training together and get a group rate on classes. But her co-workers' responses were lukewarm. They told her things like, "Oh, well, it would just take too much to learn it elsewhere." They preferred to simply wait until they had to learn it.

Betsy decided to take the initiative for the sake of her own career. She found an outside source of training and paid for it out of her own pocket. But she didn't stop there. Once she'd acquired the new skills set, she went on the hunt for a hospital that was already using the new 3D/4D technology. Not only did Betsy want to position herself where she could put her new skills to good use, she also wanted a hospital that was committed to the cutting edge of technology. She knew that such an employer would offer much more room for career growth and advancement and through that, job security.

Betsy wound up at another hospital, with a higher salary. Whatever happened to Betsy's old co-workers? They were replaced by new employees who came in already possessing the 3D/4D skills and training.

activ: *Career Steps*

Keep up with the cutting edge. If you work in a technology-driven field, you should constantly keep abreast of new advancements, equipment and skills. In fact, you should consider that to be part of your job, even if your current employer doesn't place a premium on it. Get involved in professional organizations, read trade publications, and check out what relevant courses are being offered at your local community colleges and trade schools.

Work training into your performance reviews. Annual performance reviews (or semi-annual, quarterly, etc.) are great opportunities for you to nudge your employer towards providing more technological training. When the person handling your review asks you for feedback on your position, use that time to identify the needs you see in your department, and suggest ways to develop an action plan that promotes training and growth. Not only will you improve your chances of receiving the necessary training, but by taking the initiative you may really impress your employer with your managerial and problem-solving skills!

Negotiate training into your next benefits package. These days, many parts of a job offer are negotiable, not just your salary. It's perfectly reasonable to request that a prospective employer pay for workshops, seminars and certification programs that will keep you abreast of industry advancements. (Sometimes a company will require that you work there for a year before tuition coverage or reimbursement kicks in.)

From Cornered To Corner Office

27 | *Surviving Mergers And Acquisitions*

When the hospital Drew worked at merged with another hospital, management assured everybody that this was going to be a truly balanced affiliation; no one hospital was going to take over the other. Drew's department in particular was told that they would be one of the last departments to experience change, and quite likely wouldn't have to undergo any substantial change at all.

For a while, it seemed that management had told the truth. In the weeks immediately following the merger, Drew's department sustained very little in the way of change. Looking back, Drew now sees that time as the calm before the storm.

The first big red flag came when Drew's department was told to physically move locations to clear across to the other side of the hospital building. Less than a week later, Drew's boss and almost all of his co-workers were gone. Suddenly Drew's identity was shaken to its core. Although he still had a job, he had no idea what his new role was or why he'd even been spared the ax.

Drew had thought that he might one day retire from this company, but the lies he was told after the merger changed his thinking. He resented being lied to, just as he resented that management didn't seem to think that what they did constituted lying. To them, it was about nudging along change bit by bit, giving people the truth but in a trickle-down way.

Drew went into survival mode. He didn't breathe a word of his feelings or concerns to leadership for fear of being labeled an employee resistant to change. At the same time, he found others at work who were experiencing the same trauma, and talked with them regularly as a sort of support group.

This was not the last merger or acquisition Drew would experience in his career but as the first one, it taught Drew how to survive tough transition periods and live to tell the tale. It taught him how to recognize the signs and patterns that indicate trouble down the road, so that he could prepare himself in the best ways possible. It also gave him experience he can use to help lead other co-workers through difficult transitions.

activ: *Career Steps*

Prepare. Always make sure that you have career options. Always know how the job market's doing for your particular field and where your industry is headed. Just keeping abreast of this basic knowledge will help you ready yourself in the case of unexpected change. When you know more, you can do more.

Don't play the victim. When somebody's treated you wrong, you may find yourself wanting to beat a drum to make sure everybody knows just how badly you've been treated. But if this is how you address a problem, are you giving the indication that you want positive change to come about, or are you just letting off steam and getting others to feel sorry for you? Are you really addressing the problem, or are you just addressing the emotions underneath?

Know the facts, don't assume them. In situations like a merger or acquisition, it can be hard to find the truth; even leadership's actions often don't match up with what they're saying. You have to walk the tightrope between wanting clear answers, and not wanting to look like a gossip. The best way to play detective is, first and foremost, to give others the benefit of the doubt. Gather your information from the most trusted sources you can seek out. Approach people as if they're on the same team as you, not as if you're already finding them guilty. Fact-finding is not about who to blame. It's only about finding the facts. Facts are the only thing that will serve you well during such tumultuous times.

Build alliances. When it came to seeking out emotional support, Drew was careful to speak only with others who'd been as traumatized by the merger as he had been. He didn't just start talking or gossiping with anyone who would listen. After such a sea change, it's often the case that you can build interpersonal trust with the other members of your own department or work group. In other words, seek out the company and comfort of your peers, not your higher-ups.

28 | *Wanting A Career For Which You're Not Qualified*

After Keisha was pushed out of her position as a grammar-school teacher by a difficult, unsupportive principal, she wasn't sure if she ever wanted to teach again. The school year had just ended, so she had nothing to do all summer but a lot of soul-searching. Figuring she shouldn't yet ditch the teaching field entirely and squander all that education, she decided to take a chance on a short-term position at a summer camp for disabled teens and adults.

It turned out that Keisha absolutely loved working at the camp. It not only refueled her desire to teach, but also helped her hone in on the kind of teaching she now most wanted to do, special education. She was so excited by her new career passion that towards the end of the summer, she applied for a teaching position at a public school to work with severely disabled students – even though she didn't have the specialized, state-issued certifications needed for that position.

During her interview with the school's principal, Keisha conveyed her strong desire to work with disabled kids and become a special education teacher. She spoke about her experiences at the summer camp and what she learned there. She expressed her eagerness to return to school for her required certifications, but she was just as eager to begin her career as soon as possible, ideally even before she'd earned those needed credentials.

The principal also asked Keisha about her most recent teaching position. As diplomatically as she could, Keisha spoke of the difficulties she'd encountered there. Luckily for Keisha, the interviewing principal was familiar with the principal Keisha had last worked for – and, it turned out, didn't think very highly of him.

The new principal thought she and Keisha would get along well. She was impressed by Keisha's willingness to assist students with severe disabilities. The principal made a special agreement with the state certification board, enabling her to hire Keisha on two conditions. One, Keisha would be placed under the authority of a seasoned teacher who held the needed special-ed certifications, so as to abide by state laws. Two, Keisha would complete the certifications as quickly as possible, going to school on nights, weekends and summers. Keisha agreed and her new career in special education began.

activ: *Career Steps*

Always pursue out-of-the-box opportunities. If Keisha hadn't taken a chance on the summer camp position, she never would have discovered her true career passion. Leave yourself open to volunteer opportunities, apprenticeships, and other unexpected chances to explore new fields and find out more about what you like and love. This worked for Keisha in two ways. Not only did the summer camp lead her to a specialized

From Cornered To Corner Office

career path, it also gave her needed credibility and experience in that field when it came time to look for a job.

Be prepared to make deals. Keisha was able to leverage her summer camp experience into a job interview as a special-ed teacher. Given her lack of qualifications, she had to agree to some trade-offs in order to actually land the position. Offer to return to school or agree to an initial probationary period so you can prove to your employer that you're the best person for the job.

Know why people really get hired. It's not just because they've got the right qualifications. Showing enthusiasm for the work, communicating clearly what value you bring to the organization, and connecting personally with the interviewer are three hugely important ways to make the right impression during the interview and land the position. People who hold the necessary degrees yet don't display these traits get turned down all the time. Meanwhile, someone like Keisha, who was technically underqualified, could shine in those three key ways and get hired. (Still, Keisha shouldn't have spoken badly about her last teaching position. Luckily for her, the interviewing principal happened to think just as badly of her old principal as she did.)

29 | *Curing Career Chafing*

Marilyn specialized in shifting the status quo at big corporations. Hers was a high-level position, even if it was one that existed outside a traditional company hierarchy. Her work focused on the big picture – changing an entire organization, improving the bottom line as well as overall employee satisfaction – by helping the VPs and other company leaders recognize untapped resources, new areas for growth, and ways they could make productive change throughout the company.

Marilyn loved what she did and believed in doing her job very thoroughly. So when she was hired by a food manufacturing concern to improve their management procedures, she first took six months to learn about the organization. After this period, she put together an assessment plan (summarizing the company's status quo) and drafted a proposal for change (a long-term strategy for improving the company's performance).

At her big presentation to the company brass, Marilyn shared her findings with the president and other higher-ups. The first step in her proposal was to "pick low-hanging fruit," which meant changing all the little stuff that could be modified most easily. These were changes that would be small in nature and wouldn't create a large disruption within the work environment, gently moving the organization towards new, positive transformations.

Marilyn was shocked when the president suggested that maybe they could implement just one of these "low-hanging fruit" changes within the next year! These were the tiny, painless tweaks that could all be implemented within a month. At the rate of action the president suggested, they'd be ready for some major changes in about 10 years!

By the end of the meeting, the president decided that maybe he didn't want change to come about after all. This happens all the time. Even the big kahunas around the office can get awfully frightened by change. Sometimes a manager or VP says he wants change until he sees in black and white just what that change would entail. With change comes disruption and an awkward period, and some people just aren't capable of handling that. Or a VP may say he wants change, but only if it's people below him who have to weather those changes.

Poor Marilyn went into a free fall. She spent the remainder of her stint at the company just trying to justify her paycheck. During this trying time, Marilyn started thinking long and hard about her career path. She'd been down this road before with the four companies she'd worked at previously; she'd approach a new project with enthusiasm and thoroughness only to be told, once she presented her findings, that the company didn't want change that badly after all.

Marilyn finally realized that in order to achieve different, better results in her career, she had to stop this pattern and find a way to reinvent herself and refocus her aspirations.

Today Marilyn owns her own company called The Star Makers Group. It's an organizational consulting and coaching practice that helps companies build star employees. By founding The Star Makers Group, Marilyn has solved the problems that previously plagued her career. She still deals with senior teams and company leaders to help bring an organization to the next level, but now she only takes on companies that come to her eager for change. She's narrowed her career focus, which prevents her from getting sucked into huge, long-term projects that result in relatively little improvement. Instead of dealing with whole corporations, she concentrates on individual and team development, dealing with specific employee problems rather than big-picture management issues. She's the boss, so she doesn't ever have to justify what she does to her superiors. And the best part? She still finds her work immensely rewarding.

activ: *Career Steps*

Be a visionary in your industry. In keeping abreast of your career and your field (which, as I've suggested elsewhere in this book, you should consider a regular part of your to-do list), think about how you can, or may need to, re-create and reposition yourself. Where is the untapped potential within your industry? In what ways does the industry really serve your talents and values, and in what ways does it go against them? How could you do your job differently while staying in the same industry? If Marilyn had brought up these questions to herself sooner, she would have recognized the dead-end pattern her career was taking.

Don't keep applying for the same job. When a position at one company doesn't work out, the solution is not to go out and find the same job with a different company name on it. Instead, ask yourself why you keep having to "reapply" for the same job.

From Cornered To Corner Office

30 | *Reaching The Top Of The Ladder*

Larry went to journalism school with intentions of becoming a newspaper reporter. Finding the field difficult to enter, he lucked upon a job as a copywriter at an ad agency. From there, he has steadily worked his way up the advertising ladder, moving from one agency to another.

Somewhere along the way, his career became more specialized in the area of broadcast advertising; during the latter years of his career, he stuck with agencies that focused on that niche market. Eventually, he found himself in a role as a senior executive creative director – a prestigious, enviable, high-up position.

It sounds like career success and satisfaction have always come easily to Larry. So why has he felt stalled in his career lately? It's because there's nowhere higher for him to ascend to in his current company, and he has no desire to become a company president or start his own agency. So now what?

When he thinks back on his work history, he remembers the point in time when his career turned toward television advertising. What if Larry had followed another path then, perhaps toward consumer promotion work? More importantly to his current career situation, is that a path he can viably pursue now? Larry also knows, because he's kept tabs on his industry, that interactive, web-based marketing – which wasn't even an option when he began his career – is currently a thriving market. Could he pursue a career in that area? Or maybe he could go all the way back to when he was determined to become a print journalist. Is that still a dream of his? Could that still be a viable and challenging career for him today?

To use an over-the-top analogy, think of Cher. After achieving the highest level of recognition in the field of pop music (remember Sonny and Cher?) and even reinventing her sound a few times, Cher wanted a new horizon. She turned to movie acting. While her fame afforded her the show-business connections to land movie roles, she also found she had a lot to learn about acting. Cher has often described the intimidation of walking onto the set of her first film, working alongside actors with a lot more credibility and experience. Her fame, which did get a director to take a chance on her in the first place, also placed a heavy amount of scrutiny on her performance. She could fail and be raked over the coals by critics. So why do it? One of the major reasons presumably, was her need to achieve something new, to face a new challenge. Eventually, Cher won an Oscar. She's now accepted as an accomplished actress.

activ: *Career Steps*

Accept the risk involved. The more extreme your change in careers, the more you will be "starting over." Some of the skills you've picked up along the way will translate nicely to your new career choice; others may not. You will likely not be able to start at the same high salary in a new field. This change will take an extreme commitment, but it will also provide a new journey, satisfy your ambitions and give you the challenges you need to be happy day to day. If your career is driven by challenges instead of money, this shouldn't pose much discomfort for you.

Use what you've got. Assess the skills you have, the connections you've made, and the assets that can translate to this new career path. How far will they get you? What other skills will be harder to develop? Eventually, you will have to decide whether you really want to put in the work required to "start over."

31 | *Caught In Red Tape*

When you were in college, did you ever have to transfer credits from another school, or perhaps go through the rigmarole of switching your declared major? One person at one office told you one thing about the paperwork you needed, then another person at the next office probably told you something totally opposite. You were sent down the hall, then sent down the hall again. Four more hallways and three hours later, you finally found out that you weren't even in the right building. Then you finally did find the right building and the right office, only to discover that you'd filled out the wrong forms. Just thinking back on it probably makes you want to scream.

Well, let's talk about Milton. Milton lived and worked in Illinois as an L.C.P.C. (licensed clinical professional counselor), a line of work similar to a therapist. When he moved one state away to Missouri – partly because there were more career opportunities there for him, and he dreamed of one day opening his own practice – he needed to get his license transferred. He began the process of filing paperwork with Missouri's state registry office. He encountered nothing but red tape and roadblocks at every step. Over two and a half years, he made infinite phone calls to find out exactly what he needed to do to have his Illinois license grandfathered in, and in return received about a dozen conflicting letters from the state registry office. He paid four different application fees at $100 each, and he enrolled in and paid for four different graduate courses that he was told he'd need in order to secure a Missouri license.

During this entire time, he was employed by a behavioral health concern in Missouri that worked with mentally disabled clients, but he could never work at his full capacity because he still didn't possess the proper credentials. He was passed over for promotions and missed out on additional income.

After weathering all of this, Milton found out through the National Board for Certified Counselors that there was a provision in place that should have allowed him to receive his Missouri license without having to take one course, or do any of the things he did for two and a half years.

How do you think Milton felt? Angry and ready to seek revenge? On the contrary. During this whole time, Milton became involved in committee work for his employer, helping to develop better business practices. At first, he did this to position himself as a valuable contributor, even though he didn't have all the credentials he needed. But in the process, he discovered that he actually preferred to do this kind of work, and in the end, he was offered a new position that didn't require the transfer of his license at all. In fact, Milton came to believe that having his own practice might not be a good match for him after all. Life presented something better during the process.

Sometimes following a process – even one we didn't want to be a part of at first – yields a different and better result. Focusing on what he could offer rather than what he couldn't provided Milton with opportunities that wouldn't have come his way if he'd gone through things feeling only anger and frustration.

activ: *Career Steps*

Find the silver lining in any career experience. In my opinion, the silver lining should always be about what you can learn from a given situation. Milton's situation was quite negative and unfair, yet he refused to let himself become a victim of his own circumstance. Instead, he looked for new avenues where he could still be productive and valuable.

Make sure the cost is worth it. As he was going through the process, Milton kept asking himself if it was worth it. He didn't let himself get caught up in the idea that it had to be worth it to go through everything he went through. Instead, he checked in with himself, and through that discovered a new career choice that he actually found more rewarding.

32 | *The Constantly Revolving Company*

itch had worked at a well-known publishing company for a very pleasant and productive two years when things began to change, and didn't stop. One day Mitch walked into work and was told out of the blue that the company was consolidating its legal publishing house with its medical publishing house. That very same day the announcement was made that Mitch's boss was being terminated.

This meant that Mitch was going to have to prove himself all over again to a new boss while trying not to react negatively to this blindsiding change. There were other changes, too: new financial approval processes, new volume-measuring reports, new HR policies. From what Mitch could see, the place had turned into a micromanaging machine that was actually hurting the company's overall productivity. What Mitch didn't know at the time was that all of these changes were being enacted in order to position the company for the auction block.

A year later, Mitch felt confident enough to approach his superiors with a positioning strategy that would put him in charge of two departments, saving the company money and providing him with career advancement possibilities. His higher-ups approved Mitch's plan, but just as he was getting ready to take the lead, the company's reporting structures were changed again. Suddenly Mitch was answering to another boss who was just recently hired. Mitch's plan was shelved and he was asked instead to choose just one department to lead, either art and design or media production.

Mitch chose art and design and after about six months he was starting to feel like his feet were firmly planted once again. Then the company was bought out by a rival publishing giant. Mitch's boss, the one who'd been there less than a year, was let go, as was the entire media production department, the department Mitch could have been leading had he not made it his second choice.

It had been a hostile takeover this time, and that hostility permeated everything the company said and did. Mitch got the hint and saw the writing on the wall. He started looking for ways to reinvent himself within the market and developed an interest in Internet design. He found ways to gain experience and knowledge in that field while still on the job. Eventually that experience and knowledge led him out of the company altogether. Mitch was delighted to receive a job offer from a leading Fortune 500 company in the field of Internet design.

And guess what? Six months after Mitch left his old publishing company, it was sold again!

activ: *Career Steps*

Don't let yourself get fooled twice. Have you heard the saying, Fool me once, shame on you, fool me twice, shame on me? That's exactly what happened to Mitch. Buyouts do occur often, but when they occur this often to the same company, there's nowhere to go but down.

Look to tweak your career focus, not completely reinvent it. For Mitch, transitioning to the field of Internet design wasn't a very large leap, since he had been working in the art and design department of a publishing house. When you need to get out of a company quickly, look for ways you can just tweak your expertise, which won't take as much time as learning a completely new skills set.

33 | *Sidelined By Role Changes*

J oyce worked in the Information Systems department at an internationally known beer company. Over the course of 15 years, she grew into a leading department manager, but thanks to constant change, it took some perseverance to get there.

Within a 10-year span of time, Joyce had worked under four different chief information officers, each with a different managing style. One was rigid and unapproachable; another easygoing, but couldn't delegate; the third a great communicator who offered autonomy and support; the last CIO felt overworked and didn't offer to spend much time with his employees. Often, with a leadership change in an organization comes a mix-up in the organization's structure. Beware: Managers and leaders tend to bring on other employees with whom they have worked well in the past.

Joyce suddenly found herself in a situation where the structure had changed and she was stripped from her management duties and given a non-management job. This caused Joyce to wonder if she was on her way out. Understandably, she felt panicked about what to do next. Should she dust off the resume after 15 years of dedication to the organization and leave on her own? Joyce kept looking for ways to continue to add value in any way she could, ultimately becoming part of a management change committee. This single move became her saving grace. Being a part of this committee allowed her to interact with the current CIO. It didn't take long until she was recognized as a valuable contributor and was offered a position as a group manager.

activ: *Career Steps*

Dig in and do the best you can with what you have. Had Joyce not taken the opportunity to be a part of the management change committee, she would have been overlooked and missed an opportunity she had no idea even existed. She most likely would have moved on to another organization, building new relationships and trying to rebuild the 15 years of established trust that she had left behind.

Here's the point: Take advantage of opportunities anywhere you can. Many other employees viewed this committee as a waste of time. Build relationships and look for ways to add value even when you feel vulnerable. Shutting down only brings discouragement and often intensifies fear of the unknown.

34 | *Not-For-Profit Vs. For-Profit*

ames had spent most of his career at small businesses when he got the chance to work for a very large, not-for-profit organization. He leapt at the chance to develop his managing expertise, something he wasn't really able to do at his old job since the company had so few employees.

For five years, the experience-gaining potential at the not-for-profit really thrilled him. He became quite adept at managing several entities simultaneously. Then the not-for-profit developed some internal struggles. Some of those entities James managed were going to be shut down entirely. He figured it was probably a good time to start looking for a job elsewhere.

When James originally joined the not-for-profit, it didn't matter to him that he was leaving the for-profit sector. What was most important was the opportunity for career expansion and growth. When he started interviewing for his next job, he didn't care whether it was with a for-profit or a not-for-profit. As it turned out, he wound up interviewing exclusively at for-profit companies, one of which offered him $15,000 more to do the exact same job he'd done at the not-for-profit! Then again, it truly was the exact same work, and James knew that the learning curve wouldn't be nearly as steep this time around. But the money was too good to pass up, so he happily accepted the job.

activ: *Career Steps*

If you need experience, don't focus on money. Look at the experience you'd gain from a lower-paying job as part of your "paid schooling." Later in your career, you can "trade up" that experience for a higher salary.

But also know when it's time to get paid for what you're worth. Part of the point of advancing in your career is to advance your salary as well. If you're a resourceful employee, as James was, you can often find ways to create your own opportunities within a high-paying position to keep yourself challenged as you see fit.

35 | *Hiring Freeze Leads To Opportunity Freeze*

J asmine loved her work as a manager for a pharmaceutical company, so when the company was bought out by a larger health-care conglomerate and word came down that there would be a yearlong hiring freeze while the organization was restructured, she chose to stick it out. She understood that the freeze didn't just mean no new hires; it also meant no transfers or promotions for existing employees. But she figured a year wasn't too long to just mark time in her career, especially since she enjoyed her work and her employers so much.

Mergers, buyouts and restructuring take place often in corporate America, and jumping ship every time they happen isn't necessarily the best game plan. But when a company-wide, no-exceptions freeze is placed not just on new hires, but on internal promotions, the idea of being "paid for performance" goes right out the window. An employee can quickly lose his or her incentive to do more and add value to the company.

The other problem with Jasmine's situation was that the one-year hiring freeze turned into a two-year hiring freeze, and then some. Jasmine remained stalled in her career, waiting for the promise of bigger and better opportunities. During that time, two different people in higher positions than Jasmine left the company. Her immediate boss told her he'd love to promote her to either of those positions, but his hands were tied. Those two missed opportunities were enough for Jasmine, and she soon left the company. Looking back, Jasmine was glad she got out when she did. It wound up taking more than three years for that conglomerate to unfreeze its hiring practices.

activ: *Career Steps*

Don't just wait; watch. Simply taking the company's word at face value wound up working against Jasmine. Instead, she should have looked for clues indicating whether that one-year promise would really hold true. Seek out evidence of active change. Are memos sent outlining the steps being taken towards a successful restructuring? Are the necessary changes being made to systems like payroll?

See who starts leaving first. Statistics have shown that when large changes take place at a company, the best performers are often the ones who exit soonest, unless leadership exhibits a real plan to retain them.

Keep your self-doubts in check. Leaving a work situation such as Jasmine's – feeling like your career has suffered due to unmet expectations – can make one feel like damaged goods. That's when it's important to do some damage control on your own sense of confidence. Telling prospective employers that you're looking for a company with opportunities for growth and advancement can only be beneficial to you.

Section 4:
Cornered By Culture

According to The Survey Institute, a healthy two-thirds of American workers would recommend their current place of employment to a friend as a good overall place to work. Perhaps that's because 70 percent of them believe that there is a high level of trust within the organization, while 75 percent believe that management is interested in the welfare of its employees.

I would recommend my company to a friend as a good overall place to work.

10%	23%	67%
Disagree	Neutral	Agree

There is a high level of trust in our organization.

13%	17%	70%
Disagree	Neutral	Agree

Management is interested in the welfare of its employees.

11% Disagree **14**% Neutral **75**% Agree

So why is it that, in the same surveys, only 58 percent of people polled claimed that management is doing a good job overall? Or that only 48 percent believe that management treats employees fairly?

Overall, management is doing a good job.

10% Disagree **32**% Neutral **58**% Agree

Management treats us fairly.

9% Disagree **43**% Neutral **48**% Agree

People often confuse good salaries and comprehensive benefit packages with being treated well. While those things are surely important, how you're treated on a day-to-day, personal basis around the office is just as important. How much you enjoy your surroundings, how well you get along with others, and how much you're allowed to thrive at work are the factors that will ultimately lead to career advancement and satisfaction. Figuring out how well you fit into your company's culture – whether your personal and professional values line up with the company's values, whether your innate strengths and talents match up with what the company looks for in a promotable employee – is perhaps the most overlooked aspect of career fulfillment.

As I've said already in this book, ultimately you are responsible for figuring out productive ways around potential roadblocks. One piece of advice to remember: Your human resources department is not necessarily your all-purpose life preserver when negotiating your way through the company-culture waters. To wit, only 50 percent of those polled by The Survey Institute believe that their company's HR department is doing a good job overall. Quite frankly, involving the HR department in any problems or disputes you might be having can easily read like you're "running to Mommy and Daddy." Finding and carrying out smart solutions to your problems will often rest on your own shoulders.

Overall, the Human Resources department is doing a good job.

16% Disagree **34%** Neutral **50%** Agree

That being said, there's an important question that you should ask yourself about your current workplace…

What is my company's "cultural currency"?

Look around your workplace. What type of individuals have been promoted in the past year? If being promoted to the next level is your goal – and if that level involves managing others – you need to evaluate how well you fit your company's manager profile.

Even though your bosses may value you in your current position (and even reward you with bonuses and raises), they may at the same time feel your work style would never fit within their leadership team. The truth is that many organizations have unspoken expectations for management positions. The higher you get within an organization, the more you're probably going to be held up to a preconceived profile. If your personality doesn't fit the definition – that is to say, if you don't have the right "currency" – you may be fighting an uphill battle to be recognized and promoted.

Sometimes, simply adjusting your focus can change how the company sees you and your potential. In other cases, *what you have to offer* may be such a mismatch with *what the company values* that you need to make the decision to move on.

Before deciding which move is right for you, take a look at the following work cultures and see if any of them sound familiar. Recognizing your work culture could be the key to the next phase of your career!

THE GRINDSTONE CULTURE

"Wow, Bob works 70 hours a week. His amazingly busy work schedule shows me that he's dedicated to this job. I think he deserves a raise and maybe even a promotion."

In a Grindstone Culture, the main thing that gets management to notice you – and *possibly promote* you – is simply working hard, long hours. *Smart thinking* is rarely discussed, and *true productivity* may not necessarily be the most important thing. In these managers' eyes, *hard work* is all that matters. Say goodbye to your personal life, because in this kind of organization, it takes a backseat to company projects and deadlines. So, the equation is simple: The more hours you work, the more likely you are to be rewarded with promotions.

The Currency Of The Grindstone Culture =
Hours spent working.

Signs Of A Grindstone Culture
- Do you hear managers praising people publicly for the number of hours they work? Does this type of praise seem to override praise

for any *other* types of performance, such as innovation, problem-solving and results delivered?

- When announcing promotions, does management emphasize the personal sacrifices made by the person being promoted?
- Does the average employee in your company work more hours than those in similar companies?
- Do managers in the company routinely change their personal plans at the last minute when work situations occur? Do they cancel or postpone vacations when time-consuming projects crop up at the last minute? Do you feel that this level of dedication is constantly expected from *you*, too?

THE POPULARITY CONTEST CULTURE

"Bob is so much fun! He really makes everyone's day, doesn't he? I think he would make a great leader."

The person destined for success in this type of work environment is easy to spot. He or she always has a joke on hand, makes funny comments during meetings, etc. They never have trouble keeping the mood light, always managing to entertain co-workers with a good laugh. Understandably, this person is Mr. or Miss Popularity in the office.

The thing is, this person's real ability and work-related results are being overshadowed by the effect he or she has on fellow team members. That's why it's no surprise that when this person is brought into a leadership role, their promotion is supported by peers.

The Currency Of The Popularity Contest Culture =
Popularity and humor.

Signs Of A Popularity Contest Culture

- Are company meetings excessively social and party-like in atmosphere? Is the social aspect of the organization highly regarded by leaders?
- Do company leaders openly praise the more charismatic and entertaining members of the team?
- Are people overly interested in who asks whom to lunch, who gets invited to whose weddings, and other social engagements that happen outside of normal work hours?

THE FLATLINE CULTURE

"Bob is so even-keeled. No matter what happens, he maintains his cool. He'd be a great addition to the management team."

Here's an environment where showing emotion *doesn't* earn you points. In The Flatline Culture, the goal is to do the most work while showing the least amount of emotion, even in a crisis. While it may be okay (or even valued) to have a mix of personalities in the organization, *outward* expressions of passion for the work tend to hold people at their current levels. Why? Because workers who show what some consider "excessive emotion" are not seen as capable of managing others.

This kind of management style breeds leaders who management "never has to worry about." So someone who becomes outwardly upset over a company failure, gets angry when treated unfairly by a peer, or even celebrates too wildly when the company gets a big win, is seen as too unpredictable to be in a leadership role. Showing a consistent, calm personality – no matter what happens – is equated with maturity and the ability to lead.

The Currency Of The Flatline Culture =

Ability to remain calm in any situation.

Signs Of A Flatline Culture

- When management discusses the company's future, do they sound somewhat flat and uninspiring? Do they praise "passion" for the business, but never walk the walk?
- When conflict occurs, do managers become excessively diplomatic? Do they make attempts at "smoothing over" the situation as opposed to determining the cause of the conflict?
- When the company underperforms (not meeting projections, for example), does management go overboard in telling everyone "everything will be okay"? Do you feel like you and your co-workers are more concerned than management is when it comes to these failures?

THE AHA CULTURE

"Bob came up with an answer that no one else thought of. He's always thinking! We need him to be more involved with management."

Companies are always looking for new, innovative ways to achieve success. The Aha Culture grows where organizations value innovation above all. Often in this kind of culture, mundane or seemingly obvious solutions are seen as "old school." True innovation – or even the *appearance* of innovation – is what gets people recognized.

The person who succeeds in this environment is constantly challenging the status quo and coming up with big ideas for how to do things differently. Many Aha Cultures don't worry about how many of a worker's ideas end up being scrapped because of cost or infeasibility; just the fact that they conceived something so different elevates this person's profile within the organization. Here's the irony: The "innovators" are often promoted to management, where they usually end up spending more time "managing" and less time coming up with new ideas.

The Currency Of The Aha Culture =
Innovation (even where it's not necessarily needed).

Signs Of An Aha Culture
- Does management frequently "rethink" organizational structure? Is your company in a constant state of restructuring?
- Do major internal company initiatives often lose momentum and fade away before completion?
- Does your company have a tangible program in place for rewarding innovation in the company? If so, do the ideas they reward ever become a reality, or are they discussed, honored and never heard of again?

THE CONFORMITY CULTURE

"It didn't take Bob long at all to fit in here. He caught on to what we are really about quicker than anyone we've seen yet. I think he's definitely management material."

You know what they say, If it ain't broke, don't fix it. This type of culture truly lives this sentiment, placing a high value on a company's traditional processes and achievements. Understandably, management reveres the procedures and methods that they created to sustain the company.

Sure, they might say change is important, but it's often secretly feared by those in power. Why? Because they want to maintain the status quo. As the market forces changes in their product, their technology and even their company structure, they crave the comfort of continuity; it's gotten them this far, why should they stop now? So they look around the organization and reward the ones who follow rather than lead – the ones who "get" how the organization functions. At its most extreme, this culture seems determined to promote clones of current senior management, whatever their guiding characteristics happen to be.

The Currency Of The Conformity Culture =
Not rocking the boat.

Signs Of A Conformity Culture
- Does there seem to be a "uniform" among the managers in the company? Does it seem they all shop at the same store when it comes to personal fashion?
- Do workers talk about their personal passions and hobbies, or do they just talk about work-related issues? Do their managers ever talk about personal passions or almost exclusively about work?
- Do the members of the senior management team belong to the same kinds of organizations or clubs?
- If there is a company-supported charity, is there an unspoken stigma attached to anyone who doesn't choose to support that charity?

THE PROCESS CULTURE

"Bob really gets how we handle things here. We should put him into a position to teach our processes to others."

Believe it or not, sometimes all it takes is to cross all the Ts and dot all the Is to make it up the corporate ladder. In this kind of culture, "following the rules" is seen as a cornerstone to doing great work. Closely related to The Conformity Culture, this type of company is more willing to tolerate various personalities – perhaps even celebrate diversity of personalities in their organization – as long as each follows procedures. These companies usually have incentives in place for doing things by the book.

The Currency Of The Process Culture =
Obeying procedures.

Signs Of A Process Culture

- Does the company have an incentive program in place for following procedures or meeting deadlines, but none in place rewarding quality of contribution or innovation?
- Are the highest-level managers left-brained, analytical types who make decisions after heavy analysis instead of through intuition?
- Are all new company initiatives undertaken after exhaustive research and lengthy committee discussion?

THE PIGEONHOLE CULTURE

"Bob comes to us with 10 years of field experience – exactly what we outlined in the job description."

Sometimes a company knows – or thinks it knows – exactly what it's looking for in a leader. A Pigeonhole Culture defines its open positions very specifically. They tend to be unwilling to depart from any single point in their position definition – even when an otherwise exceptional candidate comes along!

This kind of culture can also be reluctant to promote from within. The unwritten belief is that most, if not all, of the current employees are well-placed. While it's not impossible to be promoted within the organization, employees must realize that the company tends to pigeon-hole them in their current role.

To break free from this rigid structure (especially to a position for which you do not have *all* the experience required in the strict job description) can take a lot of work and "campaigning." You see, management tends to be less receptive to internal candidates than to those coming from their recruiters and "headhunters."

There are two realities to face when working in this type of organization. First, if you are a star performer in your current role, management and HR should work very hard to keep you in that position; this could include substantial incentives and raises. HR will often do whatever they need to keep you in your current position, because you do it well. The second reality you must face is that you may have no choice but to look outside the company when you become restless and ready to move ahead. It's sad but true: Employers may be unable to think outside the box enough to see you doing a different job.

The Currency Of The Pigeonhole Culture =
Outside experience.

Signs Of A Pigeonhole Culture

- Are almost all high-level positions filled from outside the company?
- Does HR ever break from the strict description of a position when hiring or promoting? Do they disqualify candidates because of small details that keep them from fitting the exact job description?
- Does senior management seem overly enamored with how long someone has been in the industry versus what they've actually accomplished along the way?

- Does the company offer training or education to learn the skills that are necessary to advance in your career, or is all training focused on improving performance in the job you already hold?

Hopefully, these company culture descriptions relate how the leadership in a company can develop a very precise and preconceived idea of what promotable employees look like, sound like and even how they behave. Again, most companies claim to value diversity in their management team, but not all organizations do. If you don't fit their "mold," you may not be seen as having management potential.

Often, the factor that is holding you back may be something that is so inherently a part of you that you can't change it. If so, you must question whether your current company is really a place where you can advance in your career.

This is key: You must understand that a failure to fit your company's management mold is not necessarily *your* failure. For example, you shouldn't blame yourself if you're looking for better ways to accomplish a job when your company secretly values conforming to old-school methods. Perhaps you should pack up your experience, knowledge and ideas and market yourself to a company that values innovation – not out of spite, but because it's a better fit for your personal assets.

It's also important not to blame the company or its leaders for their culture. While you may not agree with how people are chosen for promotion, you must respect the choices of the leaders if those choices have helped the company prosper. There are many paths to success, and your company may have simply chosen one that does not allow a person like yourself to really share in the journey as a leader.

Finding a great employer is almost like dating to find "the one." You must find the perfect marriage for *you*. Remember, the company culture that fits you may be very different from one that fits someone else who is equally dedicated, capable and talented. Two people with the same job skills, experience and knowledge can still be very different when it comes to the type of company in which they can find the most success.

Determine what kind of culture attracts you the most, then think about whether or not you are already there. Does your current employer value you beyond what you're doing at the moment? Are you the type of person they see as management material? If not, do you currently have the "currency" to succeed in the kind of culture in which you desire to work? These are the kinds of questions you should be asking yourself in order to find the perfect work culture for you.

Source: Statistics provided by The Survey Institute.

36 | *Handcuffed By Hierarchy*

F rank was a young man who didn't like his job. The main reason? It wasn't utilizing his strengths to his maximum capacity. Frank enjoyed working with and helping others. What Frank struggled with were things like prefabricated rules and regulations, as well as the corporate politics that limited what he could and couldn't do in his role within the human resources department.

All the rules set in place by the company stifled his creativity. For example, Frank once created a very comprehensive HR audit process, a development that nobody else in the department had previously built or put into practice. Frank believed it would provide more interaction with the field employees, as well as give HR the necessary regulatory information it needed.

Frank created the audit process on his own, with some input from his peers. When he presented the tool at a staff meeting, which included the company's executive vice president, she criticized it and said that HR couldn't use it. The only reason Frank could surmise was that the process was created without her input and without a direct initiative given by her. His tool wasn't rejected because it was poorly designed; it was rejected because he didn't go through the proper channels to get permission to design it in the first place.

Frank's office environment embraced a "process culture." Following preestablished rules and processes overruled almost all other factors, including creativity and innovation, in defining "success."

Cut to six months later, the end of the year approaching. Only then did the HR staff discover that they would have to clean up the database manually, and fast, before the year ended. This time-consuming process could have been avoided if they had implemented Frank's proposed audit tool back in the spring!

activ: *Career Steps*

Understand that every workplace has its politics. Upon taking a new job, find out quickly what spoken or unspoken rules govern the place. For example, some companies are very open about their internal organizational hierarchy: who reports to whom, how management is structured, or which channels new rules and processes must pass through before they can be okayed and implemented. Other companies are very closed-off about such things and don't really make their hierarchies known. Likewise, some higher-ups give their employees chances and room galore to make mistakes and learn from them, while others adhere to a strict three-strikes-and-you're-out policy.

Observe how business is done and look for who "holds the keys," so to speak; that is, who is the real *decision maker. What might surprise you is that it's not always the top dog! Take note of which people make decisions that go beyond the normal scope of their job descriptions. At meetings, look for which employees are allowed more autonomy to speak and make suggestions in front of their superiors.*

Present choices. Often you get a better outcome if you offer an array of solutions to the decision maker. Some bosses might feel hemmed in when an employee tells them there is only one possible solution to a problem.

Keep your goals in line with company goals. If you feel that your efforts to create new processes and develop better ways of doing business fall on deaf ears, it could be that your goals do not line up with those held by the department or company. Some companies value sticking to the tried-and-true more than they value innovation. Often we think that we have great solutions, but if they don't match the director's or VP's ideals, you could find yourself doing a lot of work for nothing.

From Cornered To Corner Office

37 | *Stuck Between Union And Management*

Darren had a union job at a union plant, working as a team leader in a truck-parts factory. One day he was told by management to have his team clean up their workstations, because some corporate reps were coming for a visit.

Darren was known for being meticulous and catching details. That was one reason he was a team leader. The morning after the corporate visit, Darren was quite surprised to be approached by management and told that the three hours his team had spent cleaning their workstations was excessive. Management, in conjunction with the HR department, proceeded to "write up" Darren, putting him on a corrective action plan. Darren tried to reason with them. He said that he wasn't trying to cheat the company, only carry out the orders he was given, and that he wasn't given a time frame for the task, but they wouldn't listen.

Working in a union environment often means that if you've got any issue with anything the boss is telling you, the only way to solve the problem or make yourself heard is to get your union spokesperson involved. Darren was forced to go to his shop steward (aka, the union spokesperson) to make his appeal. He explained that his team was clocked in on their non-production time cards (as opposed to the time cards that count their hours doing actual assembly work on the line) while they cleaned their workstations. Darren managed to convince the shop steward that considering he hadn't been given specific time constraints to accomplish the task, he'd carried out the orders to the best of his abilities. The steward took up the issue from there, and Darren managed to avoid the corrective action, which could have stalled Darren's career progress or salary increases down the road.

activ: *Career Steps*

Think of your spokesperson as your lawyer. Your union spokesperson is your representation in the eyes of the company. Let that spokesperson do the work and the talking for you. Rather than trying to argue a case yourself, defer to your spokesperson. Always have your spokesperson's phone number handy, and know how to get ahold of him or her quickly.

Gather more information than you need. If you were in a car accident, you wouldn't just take down the other person's phone number and then leave the scene. You'd call in the police, explain what happened, take pictures, etc. Document and put into writing whatever you can, should you need that proof for a case down the road.

Decide how badly you need a mouthpiece. A union will pre-negotiate your starting salary and benefits, and almost always, those will be higher and better than what a non-union worker in the same industry will get. However, when you join a union, you're also giving up some of your autonomy and your rights to negotiate on your own behalf. Some people do well in a union environment, others find it rubs them the wrong way. You can always speak to a friend who's in a union to get a more personal sense of the ups and downs.

From Cornered To Corner Office

38 | *Sticking Out Socially*

Mary's first job out of college was at a cable TV show in New York. She was very excited about it and felt like she deserved it; she'd earned a minor in film and video production at school, and she'd interned at two other TV programs while still an undergraduate. She definitely felt ready to embark on a career in television.

Mary's job was as a production assistant, which basically meant she did all the grunt work: running errands, making copies, sending faxes, answering phones, picking up lunches, etc. Even though the work was far from stimulating, Mary enjoyed her position immensely. She got along very well with the other PAs, many of whom were also young and new to the paid workforce, and with the show's writers, many of whom moonlighted as stand-up comedians. "I literally work with a bunch of comedians!" Mary loved saying to her friends.

Mary was the sort of girl who was always smiling and making jokes, and who possessed a loud, boisterous laugh – traits that, she assumed, made her a perfect fit for working on a comedy show. So you can imagine how shocked Mary was when three months into the job, she was ushered into the executive producer's office and told she was being let go.

Mary immediately asked why. The executive producer told her, "It's clear that you're not interested in doing the dirty work. You're just in this for the fun and the glamour." Mary was so stunned she could barely manage a response. She explained to her boss that she was diligent about doing all the tasks she was given, but her boss had clearly already made up her mind. Mary was escorted out of the building that night.

It took Mary years to finally realize what the problem had been at her first job. While the other PAs may have been young and personable like her, and while the writers/comedians may have appreciated her sense of humor, she had unknowingly been giving off a bad impression to the higher-ups the whole time. They interpreted Mary's demeanor around the office as goofing off. They assumed she didn't take her work seriously. Though Mary got along easily with those co-workers who were low on the totem pole like she was, she hadn't given any thought to what it took to make a good impression with the people who mattered most – the ones who could promote her or ultimately, fire her.

activ: *Career Steps*

Learn the golden rule of office politics: Perception is reality. The impression that you give off at work is just as important as the actual work you are doing. Those who worked down in the trenches with Mary could see that she was putting great effort into her duties, but what the executive producer saw (from afar) was a young girl who didn't seem to take her job seriously.

Hunker down during crunch times. When the company's got a deadline to hit, it's not the time to crack jokes. You may think you're helping out by lightening the mood, but the higher-ups, the ones whose reputations are on the line, may very well view your levity as downright insubordination. Besides, it's not your job to set the tone for the whole office. Instead, just smile warmly and be as helpful and productive as you can until the storm passes.

Read your boss' emotional cues. This is where your boss' assistant can really help you out. Before you approach your boss to discuss something important, check in with the assistant to find out how he or she is feeling that day. Then fine-tune your demeanor so that it's in line with the demeanor of your boss. The boss will feel like you're really on his or her team.

At the same time, it's important to remember to lighten up every once in a while. Depending on the industry and the office, some workplaces can be almost alarmingly laid-back and social. If you come from a straitlaced, buttoned-down work background, you may find yourself in a situation opposite Mary's: being looked over for promotions because the company values people-friendly, outgoing employees. There are plenty of little steps you can take to thaw the ice with your co-workers. Invite an associate out for a drink after work, take your wardrobe cues from your boss, or share something interesting or funny about a real-life experience.

39 | *The Lazy, Underachieving Workplace*

One summer Stan worked as a custodian for the local school district. On paper his job description was to work with a team of three others at an elementary school, cleaning every desk, room and drawer and doing maintenance work such as stripping floors, putting new wax down, etc.

Soon after taking this new job, Stan realized there wasn't enough work to keep the four of them busy. Really, they could have taken care of all their work within a month's time, but the job was scheduled to last two months. Stan would report in at 8 a.m. only to drink coffee and listen to his co-workers dish about their personal lives. (What they were involved in can't be mentioned in this book!)

Feeling stuck and frustrated, Stan tried to encourage everyone to work a little bit harder in the mornings, instead of talking or sleeping the first couple of hours away. His suggestions were met with nothing but resistance from his colleagues, and when he tried to do work on his own they scolded him for making them look bad!

The supervisor, Nick, was getting close to retirement; he didn't want a newcomer barging in and changing the way work got done (or didn't get done, as the case may be). Though Nick was on-site with his employees the whole time, he really didn't seem to care whether or not the work was completed quickly. Nick was well-liked by his employees, largely because he didn't believe in "tattling" on the job. Obviously, when Stan went to Nick with his concerns, he got no help from him. The philosophy at play was clear. Do as little work as possible, just enough so nobody can point a finger at you.

Isn't it amazing to think that these people were probably spending more energy avoiding work than they would have spent if they just did the work in the first place?

Ultimately, Stan decided to just finish out his time at the job and keep busy as best he could. Since it was a short-term position, it wasn't worth his energy and efforts to try to improve things. But after that experience, Stan realized how stuck he'd feel if he ever wound up in a similar position again. Stan vowed to never again get involved in a workplace where he couldn't give 100 percent.

activ: *Career Steps*

Always interview the company for the right fit. Clearly, Stan was the sort of person who valued hard work and making a contribution. When he was applying for the job, he could have asked, "What does a regular day on the job look like?" If the interviewer hems and haws when giving his answer, there's a good chance that productivity isn't high on his agenda. During the interview process, try to meet face-to-face with the superior you'll be working with most closely and reporting to most regularly. Does his or her personality seem a little too laid-back? Does he or she give vague, general answers to your questions, or do you get specific responses?

Don't be afraid to go higher. Stan probably had more choices than he thought. He could have gone above Nick to the superintendent's office to voice his concerns. While your immediate boss may not care about producing value for the company, somebody higher up probably wants to know that the company's not getting the best bang for its buck.

Know when to quit pushing the rock up the hill. If you sense that a lazy attitude is permeating every aspect of the job, you're probably better off leaving the company than possibly sabotaging your career. (Especially if, unlike Stan, you're in a full-time, long-term position with no quick-exit strategy.) You should have no problem interviewing with other companies and telling them you're looking for a more challenging work environment. What employer wouldn't love to hear that?

From Cornered To Corner Office

40 | *The Stepchild Contractor*

A "contract employee" is like the temp of the new millennium. In the 1990s, temps were an extremely cost-efficient way for companies to fill busywork roles without paying full benefits or devoting time and energy to screening, hiring and orienting new workers. Compared to the temps of yesterday, today's contract employees actually have it a little better. Like a temp, a contract employee is placed into a company by an outside firm, but it's usually on a long-term basis instead of day-to-day or week-to-week, and it's often to work on a specialized project, rather than simply to do grunt work.

But still, contract employees are rarely considered "part of the family," especially within larger companies. Because of this, their opinions and expertise, not to mention their career potential, are often ignored by the people for whom they're producing value.

As one of three contract employees working in a company's organizational development department, Jon really didn't get much respect from anybody. Not only was he a contractor, but he worked in a department that the VPs considered unnecessary and costly. (Organizational development deals with team leadership and employee interaction, "soft skills" that don't improve the bottom line in any immediate, measurable way.) To make matters worse, Jon's boss, the director of training, had been transferred into that role despite having no OD experience, which goes to show just how poorly the department was regarded. Even though Jon and his two fellow contract employees all possessed OD experience, the value of that experience wasn't recognized by any member of the company's hierarchy.

Jon and his fellow contractors used to joke with one another that they were treated like proverbial pond scum. Since there were no full-timers in OD, they did all of the department's work, while the credit was always given to the director of training – who, unlike them, was a "member of the family" – for his supposedly great leadership. Meanwhile, when the director would address large groups of employees (a significant part of his job) he proved so bad at delivering powerful presentations that people often fell asleep! Jon and his fellow contractors tried to suggest ways the director could improve his style, but found that he didn't care about their opinions since they were "only" contractors.

Ultimately, each of the three contract employees found ways to get unstuck from their situation. Peggy changed her career focus and landed a full-time position within a different department. Cheri left for a full-time job at a different organization that "walked their talk" when it came to valuing the work of an organizational development department. Jon went on to work for a college that allowed and encouraged individual development. He got excellent work experience as well as certifications that advanced his career. Eventually, he was offered a position at a Fortune 500 company, which he happily accepted.

activ: *Career Steps*

Seek out the good contract-employee placement firms. When dealing with a placement firm, ask questions to get a sense of the firm's focus. Does the firm specialize in HR, IT, etc.? Does it operate merely as a temp service, or does the firm truly seek to place people in positions that can lead to full-time employment? Oftentimes these firms really do want you to get hired by the companies with which they place you, because it means a bigger commission for them. You should also ask for the names of people they've recently placed, and contact them as references. Are they happy with their placement? Would they use this firm again? Do they think the placement can or will lead to full-time employment?

Nip "just-a-temp" notions in the bud. Once you've been placed as a contract employee, you need to convince the company that you're a valuable asset, not "just a temp." Look to perform above and beyond what's expected of you, in ways that add measurable *value to the company. Find processes you can streamline or systems you can improve that will result in lower costs, higher revenue or fewer man-hours.*

Revel in the perks of contract employment. A lot of people liken contract-employee work to trying on shoes. When you're a contract employee, you're free to say at any time, "Nope, don't like it," and instantly remove yourself from the situation with a simple phone call to your placement firm. If you're at a stage in your career where you're not sure what to do next, "trying on" different jobs and companies could prove to be a wonderful, enlightening experience.

Work your way inside the company. When you've found a company where you want to stay, your first move should be to make your desires known to somebody inside the company, such as an HR person. Don't go back and tell your placement firm. They're not the ones who can hire you; you'll only be reestablishing yourself as someone who's not really a member of the family. When a company sees a good temp in its midst, if they can make the hire happen, they will. Oftentimes companies have a policy that current employees get "first dibs" at an open position. As a contract employee, you don't count as an employee, but you can still position yourself so that, at the least, you're second in line.

41 | *The Unethical Workplace*

Thanks to the office gossip mill at a creative services company, it was common knowledge that Bill's boss kept a mistress on the side. Though Bill didn't particularly admire his boss' lifestyle choice, he never let it affect his work or his on-the-job attitude. That is, until Bill discovered something else about his boss. He was turning in false expense reports.

It was Bill's responsibility to process his boss' expense reports and submit them to the accounting department. In handling those reports, Bill noticed a number of unexplained costs, as well as receipts from locations the boss hadn't visited on business. Bill could tell that his boss was taking his mistress on vacations and declaring them as business trips.

Bill felt he had to do something to address this. He didn't want word about the expense reports getting out around the office because it could really sabotage company morale; how resentful people would feel to know that as they were working to create value for the company, Bill's boss was taking it away! Also, like most people, Bill tried to live by his morals, and what his boss was doing went against Bill's own ethics. He decided to approach the owner of the company and report his boss' dishonest practices.

After hearing what Bill had to say, the owner replied, "Bill, I'm so glad you brought this to my attention." Bill left the meeting feeling he'd done the right thing and that the problem would be addressed. But not three months later, Bill found the same thing happening with his boss' expense reports! He decided to talk to the owner once more.

This meeting with the owner was different. Bill could tell that the owner was trying to placate him just to get him out of his office. Suddenly, Bill was able to read the writing on the wall. There was a boys' club mentality at the company, one with an unspoken agreement: When you reach a certain level of power, it's okay to cheat a little bit. You're rewarded with such under-the-table perks.

Bill knew after that meeting that there was no point in worrying about his boss' dishonesty. It wasn't outright illegal, and the owner was silently sanctioning it. It wasn't long before Bill left for another creative services company, where he's stayed for more than 15 years. He is now an executive VP there, and he makes sure that honesty is what's upheld and rewarded.

activ: *Career Steps*

Learn the unspoken ins and outs of the company. When you're interviewing with a company, find out about its reputation within the business community. See if you can talk to former employees, and research what's been written about the company in business magazines or in the business section of your local paper. To find out more about a company you're already employed by, take a close, hard look at how and why individuals are rewarded, whether through promotions or less obvious perks, like being allowed to keep shorter hours or charge questionable expenses to the company.

Handle whistle-blowing with discretion and respect. Say you find out about unsavory business practices at your company. You could choose to handle that by handing out flyers in the lunchroom, but what outcome would you get? By telling lots of people, your apparent objective is to make someone else look bad, not to create real change from within. As a first step, it's always better to speak privately with a manager who can actually do something about the problem. Taking your message public, or to those who don't have the power to change it, is only going to create gossip.

Balance your options carefully. What would be the consequences if I told the truth? What would be the consequences if I just kept my mouth shut? Could I live with myself if I didn't do anything about this problem? Should I just leave the company altogether? There can be countless variables to a situation like Bill's, so you really need to think long and hard about what course of action to take. Living by one's own ethics is important, and there's never a time when you should just throw those out the window. But life is not black and white, so your challenge is how to maintain your standards of right and wrong while living in an unperfect world and perhaps, while working at a company where others don't care about them. If the situation is extremely delicate, you might want to seek outside legal counsel to help you flush out the facts and put together a reasonable approach.

Don't whistle-blow as a career move. Never think that ratting out or pointing the finger at somebody else is a good way to bargain for a promotion or to bring praise and glory upon yourself. If that is your only motive for whistle-blowing, it's extremely likely to blow up in your face.

42 | *Getting In With The Wrong Crowd*

Sometimes the atmosphere around the office can change drastically from department to department; sometimes your job performance may not matter as much as your social status, at least in the eyes of those with the power to promote you. These two circumstances together happened to Kiley, who worked at a customer-service call center. For his first several months on the job, he worked the day shift, where everything was done by the book. Then he was reassigned to the evening shift, only to find that evening management believed in a completely different kind of work environment. They cared about getting the work done, but didn't care as much about following policies and procedures in order to make that happen. Kiley's evening manager, for example, rewarded employees who met their quotas by giving them extra time off, an effective incentive even if it didn't align with company rules.

Kiley really enjoyed the less rigid work environment of the evening shift, not because he disliked rules or lacked discipline, but simply because he found himself better able to thrive when given some freer parameters. The problem was that Kiley wanted a promotion, and those were only given by the day-shift management. Kiley was well-liked by the night-shift managers and regularly exceeded their expectations, but since the day-shift managers were more highly regarded in the company hierarchy, that didn't matter. In fact, Kiley knew that his good rapport with the night-shift managers might ultimately count against him.

A similar situation once happened to Don, who had given his two-week notice in the IT department of a manufacturing company when a co-worker suggested he apply for an IT opening on the night shift, working Monday through Friday from 10 p.m. to 7 a.m. Don applied, got the job and happily accepted it, anticipating the sort of learning opportunities he hadn't found in his old department.

Even though Don was able to greatly broaden his skills set on the job, he found himself consistently unable to please his boss. The boss worked during the day, so Don wasn't afforded much face-to-face interaction with him. After talking about this problem with some of his co-workers, Don also learned that this particular boss greatly favored those employees he'd hired personally. Don, unfortunately, had joined the department when the boss was away on a six-month project.

In the end, Kiley had better luck getting unstuck than Don did. Don toiled away under his unreceptive boss for two years before finally securing a move to a new department. Kiley, meanwhile, saw an opportunity for himself when he learned that one of his night managers was going to be promoted to a day manager position. He confided to the manager, who was very understanding, his own goals of getting promoted. The two worked out a plan in which the manager would slowly profile Kiley's talents to the day-shift management team. It wasn't long before Kiley received the promotion he'd been wanting.

activ: *Career Steps*

Partner with the right leaders. Sometimes we can't help "falling in with the wrong crowd" at work. We may just get along better on a personal level with some people more than others. But regardless of what friendships form naturally, you must make conscious efforts to form respectful working relationships with people to whom you can make contributions, and who will be able to help your career down the road.

Don't be afraid to ask for help. Had Kiley not chosen to approach and confide in his night manager, he probably never would've gotten the promotion he wanted. People have a natural inclination to want to help others when they can and know it will be appreciated.

Seek out common causes. When looking to align yourself with the right higher-ups at work, find out what things those people care about most. Some value accuracy above all else, others place a premium on time management. With some bosses, a little bit of small talk goes a long way towards building a foundation of friendship; others find socializing distracting and annoying. People promote others when they think they'll make the same decisions as they do. It's kind of like parenting. The parent knows to cut the strings when the child can make the right decisions on his own. Building that trust will help build your opportunities.

Don't get lost in the dark. Make sure you're seen around the workplace – especially if, like Don, you work a different shift than your boss does. Face-to-face interaction is always the best and fastest way to build relationships at work. Whenever you can, speak to your colleagues and higher-ups face-to-face instead of by phone or e-mail.

43 | *Orders That Stick*

S tewart was a lieutenant in the military. He worked a desk job overseeing the purchasing department's communications inventory. That meant he assessed the military's need to make communications more effective through computers, cell phones and other devices.

Stewart had been working on the job for about two years when he started noticing the military could save money by changing some of its vendors and fixing some of its broken equipment rather than just buying new. He approached his colonel with his ideas, but the colonel was not receptive at all. He cut Stewart off before he could even finish sharing his suggestions.

Over the course of the next several months Stewart tried numerous times to tactfully push his ideas, but they were always met with resistance. In the military you are expected to follow the orders of your superiors to the letter. Questioning authority and rocking the boat are not part of the game. As long as what's being done is not illegal or immoral, you are expected to follow the orders given.

But once Stewart finished his time at the rank of lieutenant, he found that he was able to make such appeals much more successfully. In the eyes of Stewart's superiors, he had then paid his dues and earned the right to be heard. Stewart was happy that he'd been patient and that he was finally able to make more valuable contributions.

activ: *Career Steps*

Never take it personally. When it comes to the military, deferring to your superiors' orders is considered a necessary part of the job. It's how you show respect and earn trust and loyalty. While the military may be an extreme example, there are many office environments where such deference can actually get you far in the long run.

Once the colonel was convinced that the lieutenant would follow his orders to the letter of the law, the lieutenant had earned a right to be heard. Years later he was able to be a real influence on the colonel. Within some company environments, earning a right to be heard is like being given the right of passage, sometimes it just takes blood, sweat and tears.

44 | *The Go-Nowhere Career*

Suzy entered the workforce right out of college and landed what seemed to be the job of a lifetime. She was hired to work on client and vendor relations for a well-respected brewery. The culture of Suzy's department was all about socializing, and the perks of her position were ideal for a 22 year old: going to ball games and concerts, entertaining clients, drinking for free – and getting paid for it!

Perhaps even better than the perks though, was that the job seemed to hold plenty of promise and opportunity. Without even really trying, she was promoted four times during her first four years. That was part of the department's culture too. Rewards were doled out easily and generously to employees. Simply doing the job was regarded as reason for advancement, yet once you were given a promotion in title and salary, you just kept right on doing the same job you always did!

It was at this point that Suzy began to look at her colleagues and realize that she didn't want to be like them. They seemed too satisfied with the status quo, not actively pursuing new challenges, and appeared unconcerned about professional development. It looked as if there were no supervisors who might help give Suzy career direction or guide her advancement in the company. Suzy began to wonder where she would or could go from there.

Though on the surface the job appeared to contain all the elements of a fun and fantastic career, Suzy needed something with more depth, purpose and challenge. This was not a job that would help her make the mark she wanted to leave in life.

Suzy began applying in earnest at other companies. During interviews she talked with drive and passion about her desire to build a career. Eventually she found a marketing position at a foods company where she could work tirelessly, which she happily did.

activ: *Career Steps*

Know where you stand within an organization. The way things worked in Suzy's client relations department, the employees would wait around for somebody to give them feedback about their jobs. It was a very passive work culture, a good sign that there would be little opportunity for Suzy anywhere in the corporation. Stay in charge of your career path and growth, and if you don't get feedback, ask for it.

Ask yourself what you're learning from this experience. If you're not moving forward, or even if you're just standing still, then in reality your career is losing ground and moving backwards.

45 | *Hard Work Vs. Soft Skills*

When a major Fortune 500 company brought aboard a new president, one of her goals was to increase productivity. To achieve this, she envisioned a new and improved company culture, one in which managers, supervisors and directors listened to their front-line workers more closely, molded their employees into more effective team players, and relied on "emotional intelligence" to better guide their managing techniques.

The president hired Jake, a known expert in the field of organizational development, to lead the charge. Jake was asked to design and implement a weeklong boot camp for the company's leaders, taking them through a series of self-evaluations and group exercises that would lead to changes in their personal behaviors, thereby beginning the process of changing the company's culture.

The boot camp was very well-received by those who participated. Around the office, people started talking about how they felt it was making a difference in their day-to-day work lives.

Here was the unseen problem. The company's five vice presidents, who had been around since the "old regime," didn't believe that addressing employees' "soft skills" would in any way improve the bottom line. They believed that the company was built on hard work, not soft skills. It didn't take them long to successfully pressure the new president into stepping down. Soon after she went, Jake's position at the company vanished too.

activ: *Career Steps*

Don't try to build your career on shaky ground. When a company is going through a transition period, such as the induction of a new president, then nothing you're doing at your job is set in stone. Your career focus, or the company's focus, could change in an instant. While the president certainly provided Jake with a nice work opportunity, he should have been more aware of the fact that her lack of tenure at the company could've spelled trouble.

Recognize the signs of a company that favors "hard work" over "soft skills." Is the bottom line praised above all and regarded as the only indicator of a company's well-being? Does the company traditionally provide any sort of employee-relations seminars? Are promotions granted for being a good manager to employees, or for being a good manager of the company's product?

Conclusion

From Downfalls To Windfalls:
Bouncing Forward After
Hitting The Bottom

There are no guarantees in life, or in careers. In both, there will always be pit stops and potholes. You can follow all the advice in this book, spot all the potential roadblocks coming at you, take steps to remedy them in the best way possible, and at times you will still find yourself stuck. Perhaps stuck in a job you know you've got to leave. Perhaps even stuck without a job.

But that's okay. Sometimes the process of building a career means going without for a while – without a paycheck, without any chance of promotion, without any opportunities for fueling your passion – in order to ultimately create something new.

I know the feelings that come with this. Oftentimes you find yourself thinking self-defeating, negative thoughts. But I also know one thing for sure. You cannot lose your perspective or your sense of humor. They will bring you through the downtimes with flying colors.

Let me tell you about my friend Stacy. After many, many years spent working her way up the corporate ladder, she reached nirvana: the right job, a super boss, absolutely wonderful pay, awesome benefits, great staff, working in a swank section of the St. Louis metropolitan area. Life was good. And it stayed that way, at least for a while.

Then came the dreaded day when she was told that as a result of a business decision, her job – as a matter of fact, her entire department – was being eliminated. Stacy had worked hard and performed well, and it was all over. Just like that.

To ease her pain and get a perspective on things, Stacy went to lunch with a friend, one with whom she could share any thoughts and receive completely honest answers in return. That friend was me.

Stacy arrived for lunch fully prepared to vent her spleen to me, raging against all the injustices she'd encountered on the job front. In return, she expected a pep talk about how talented she was, what a fantastic skills set she possessed, and how there was definitely another job out there that was perfect for her.

It was a beautiful spring day, so we decided to dine on the restaurant's patio. Stacy started sharing her feelings of frustration, shock and disbelief when both of us heard a cracking sound. The sound happened again, louder, and then I started to feel small pieces of plastic hitting me in the back of the head. I turned around ever so slowly, just in time to see all four legs of a plastic patio chair break into a million little pieces beneath a large woman.

Stacy and I watched in amazement and awe as this woman crawled off the patio with the chair's seat and arms still stuck to her backside. It seemed as if the silence on the patio lasted forever. Finally, I turned back around to Stacy and whispered, "Well, you would think her husband could've at least helped her with the chair. Geez, we thought you were having a bad day!"

This episode was probably the most embarrassing moment of this poor woman's life. It reminded Stacy of life's important lessons, which apply to our careers as well. No matter how bad your day may be, someone out there has it worse. Sometimes you have no control over what might happen. And situations are only temporary, whether you are a lady crawling off a patio with a plastic chair stuck to your backside, a person stuck in a career rut, or a person without a job at all.

Stacy bounced back, of course, and has a fabulous career once more, complete with the super boss, wonderful pay, awesome benefits and so on. Her once-dreadful feelings of despair and disbelief are but a memory.

If you're like most people, you spend the majority of your waking hours trying to keep everybody else happy: the boss, the co-worker, the shareholder, the spouse, the kids, the in-laws, the dog. So when you find yourself in a career rut or gap, my advice is to allow yourself a little "I time." Go stroll a park, get some extra sleep, or read a good book. Give yourself permission to pull back for a little while. Even if you're still working at the dead-end job, find little ways to scale back your efforts there to give yourself time and breathing space. It will prepare you mentally and emotionally for the next steps.

When people immediately plunge headfirst into a job search, they get frantic and lose perspective. They don't think they have choices. All they can think about is the pressure of finding a paycheck. This is risky behavior, because when you feel stuck and cornered, you're not in the right frame of mind to make the best choice. In fact, those feelings add an element of risk to everything you do.

You can take charge of these feelings by taking a little break, at least enough until you realize that the world isn't going to fall apart just because you hate your job or you're not employed at the moment. (In the latter situation, an emergency savings account can't hurt either.)

Until you realize that you have choices, you'll never be able to make the best choice for you. Take time to put a game plan together, to gather the information you need to best map out your next career move.

If you're without a job, your challenge is to resist the feelings of panic that may set in. If you're still with the job, your challenge is to fight any feelings of complacency. As I said at the start of this book, people will often make lame excuses for why they're staying in an awful position: "My commute only takes 10 minutes," "I get to come in later than most people," etc. These thoughts can paralyze you and ultimately sabotage your career. Rather than actively taking charge, you're just hanging around waiting for the ax to fall.

When you no longer care what you wear to work, when you buy a lottery ticket every day hoping to strike it rich so you can quit your job, when you find yourself playing the victim role rather than playing an active role, it is time to start looking elsewhere.

Start by outlining your exit plan. Ask yourself what actions you can take that can get you closer to the result you want. Then try to take at least one small step each day that will bring you closer to that result. Read an article from a trade magazine. Invite someone to lunch whose career you admire or whose industry you want to find out about. Work on your resume during your lunch hour. Attend a professional group's monthly happy hour. There are countless little things you can do that will get you where you want to go. And with each step you take, you will grow your momentum. Your positive actions will result in positive self-fulfillment.

In order to achieve something, you have to be able to visualize it. In essence, this boils down to the old adage, If you can dream it, you can do it. Don't be afraid to dream. It is how you can best visualize what you really want.

Yes, you also need to be practical in your search, but being practical does not mutually exclude allowing yourself to dream. Visualizing and dreaming are essential steps in the very practical process of building your most perfect career. Being practical doesn't mean accepting a position just because it pays well, or taking a new job for other "practical" reasons. What it means is, conduct your search, no matter how pie-in-the-sky it may seem at first, by having as much information and as many resources on your side as possible. Back up the dream with hard facts.

When I work one-on-one with a client and we build towards that person's career goals, we construct what I call A, B and C career plans. If you only have one plan and it goes belly up, you'll wind up feeling devastated. Instead, have three different plans, all geared towards your dream career, representing the different routes you might take to get there. Plan A might be creating your own position within your current company that matches many of your strengths, interests, values and talents, much like I did when I spearheaded the Seminar Support Services department back at the Institute in Basic Youth Conflict. Plan B might entail a long-range plan that ultimately gets you to your dream job, but in the meantime you're going to accept a lateral-move position that at least brings you into your dream field. Plan C might be taking a part-time job while crafting a business plan, going on exploratory interviews in your chosen field, or attending school, so you'll have the degrees necessary to compete in your chosen career field. (If you discover, for example, that your career passion is to become an eye surgeon, you're not going to get to become an eye surgeon next week.)

Some of these plans entail taking jobs that are just that – jobs; things you can do to bring in some money while you further prepare and plan for the career you really want. It's fine if you have to exercise some survival techniques during this interim period. In fact, taking a job-job just for the money can help by relieving some of the financial anxieties that come with approaching a new career path. When you don't have a job, you can get consumed by that next step of just finding *any* job to keep you financially afloat and to make you feel like you're a valuable contributor to society. But there is a flip side to taking a job-job; you don't want to get sucked into it. If you find yourself working extra hours at the job-job, for example, it's a sign that you could be losing focus on the bigger picture. The job-job is just supposed to help you along while you pursue your dream "corner office." Again, it's about finding a balance between dreaming and practicality.

Sometimes my clients carry out a Plan B or a Plan C, and at first they're wary. Taking a job just for the money seems to go against the notion of pursuing your dream. But eventually, they come to realize just how helpful and necessary such contingency plans are. Whether it takes them two months, or 10 months, or two full years of schooling and planning and building, in the end they reach the goals they've set for themselves. It's all part of the process. Follow the process. The process works, and it will lead you to your goal.

Career coaching is a growing field expressly because it's becoming a proven, effective way to work that process. Think of it this way. When you buy a house, you hire a realtor. At the gym, when you want faster, better results than you could get on your own, you hire a trainer. What pays for the house, the realtor's services, the trainer's fees? Your career.

I hope that this book serves you as a sort of career coach in paper form. If it inspires you to seek out the services of a real-life, breathing and talking career coach, whether myself or somebody else you find, then all the better for you and your career future. In any case, you should consider just the fact that you bought this book as an investment in your career and your future.

One last thing. Remember that your career, like all parts of your life, may change with the seasons. Your original goal may be to conquer the mountain in your industry. Later on, you may find yourself seeking a different kind of work/life balance, or perhaps a different industry's mountain to conquer. There will be periods when spending time with your family will matter more to you, and times when the excitement of a new career chapter will really energize you. Listen to what these winds of change are telling you. Over the course of your life, you will spend more time in your career than you will in any relationship, or in the company of your children, or perhaps even in your own bed. Your career happiness is a huge part of your overall happiness. It is the discovery of your individual purpose and one of your truest forms of self-expression, so don't be passive about it. Be active and remain in charge of it. As I say in the very title I gave my company, "activate" your career. Do the work you need to do to make your eight-hour workday work for you.

Companies and organizations hire David Hults because of his 14 years of HR experience and his expertise in working with everything from small businesses to Fortune 500 companies. He shares his knowledge as a career coach expert, speaker and trainer, and his audiences leave not only motivated but with clear action plans. David is also available for developing customized seminars for your specific needs. Some of David's most requested speeches and workshops are as follows:

KEYNOTE:

From Cornered To Corner Office
Overcoming The Most Unexpected Obstacles That Stand Between You And Your Career Dreams

FOR PEOPLE IN CAREER TRANSITION:

From Roadkill To Road Map
The 12 biggest mistakes people make in job hunting and how to avoid them.

From "Hi" To Hired
Leave the most positive and unforgettable possible impression in interviews.

From Desperation To Deal
Learn negotiation techniques to get all you deserve.

From Frustrated To Focused
Crafting a resume for fit and focus.

FOR CORPORATIONS UPGRADING THEIR WORKFORCES:

From Conflict To Collaboration
Uniting the individual strengths of a diverse team toward one goal.

From Paralyzed To Prosperous
Embracing CHANGE and making it work for you, not against you.

From Inflexible To Influential
Apply the principles of "emotional intelligence" and respond instead of react.

activ: *Career Steps*

Schedule a CAP Session (Career Action Planning Session).

If you have found yourself stuck, stalled or cornered in your career, this session will identify what's working, what needs attention and next steps. We will get to the root cause of your career pain and move you closer to the corner office that's right for you.

For more information about speeches, seminars
and scheduling a CAP Session, contact David
by visiting the following web site:

www.activ8careers.com

(Free Career Quiz Available Online)

activ:8 career coaching
making your 8 hour workday work for you.

Career Journal
Cornered By Self

_____

_____

_____

_____

_____

_____

_____

_____

_____

_____

_____

_____

Career Journal
Cornered By Others

_____

_____

_____

_____

_____

_____

_____

_____

_____

_____

_____

_____

_____

Career Journal
Cornered By Industry

_____

_____

_____

_____

_____

_____

_____

_____

_____

_____

_____

_____

_____

Career Journal
Cornered By Culture

_____

_____

_____

_____

_____

_____

_____

_____

_____

_____

_____

_____

_____